taste of home
BEST LOVED PIES

tasteofhome
BEST LOVED PIES

Senior Vice President, Editor in Chief:	Catherine Cassidy
Vice President, Executive Editor/Books:	Heidi Reuter Lloyd
Creative Director:	Ardyth Cope
Food Director:	Diane Werner RD
Senior Editor/Books:	Mark Hagen
Editor:	Amy Glander
Art Director:	Gretchen Trautman
Content Production Supervisor:	Julie Wagner
Layout Designer:	Kathy Crawford
Proofreaders:	Linne Bruskewitz, Victoria Soukup Jensen
Recipe Asset Management System:	Coleen Martin
Premedia Supervisor:	Scott Berger
Recipe Testing and Editing:	Taste of Home Test Kitchen
Food Photography:	Reiman Photo Studio
Administrative Assistant:	Barb Czysz
Cover Photo Art Director:	Rudy Krochalk
Cover Photo Photographer:	Dan Roberts
Cover Photo Set Stylist:	Dee Dee Jacq
Cover Photo Food Stylist:	Jennifer Janz

U.S. Chief Marketing Officer:	Lisa Karpinski
Vice President/Book Marketing:	Dan Fink
Creative Director/Creative Marketing:	Jim Palmen

THE READER'S DIGEST ASSOCIATION, INC.

President and Chief Executive Officer:	Mary G. Berner
President, North American Affinities:	Suzanne M. Grimes
SVP, Global Chief Marketing Officer:	Amy J. Radin

International Standard Book Number (10): 0-89821-804-7
International Standard Book Number (13): 978-0-89821-804-6
Library of Congress Control Number: 2010920478

Timeless Recipes from Trusted Home Cooks®
is a registered trademark of Reiman Media Group, Inc.

Printed in China.
1 3 5 7 9 10 8 6 4 2

©2010 Reiman Media Group, Inc.
5400 S. 60th St., Greendale WI 53129
All rights reserved.

Taste of Home is a registered trademark of
The Reader's Digest Association, Inc.

PICTURED ON FRONT COVER: Stone Fruit Pie (p. 19)
PICTURED ON TITLE PAGE: Frosty Toffee Bits Pie (p. 64)
PICTURED ON BACK COVER: Frozen Banana Split Pie (p. 59), Blueberry Cobbler (p. 102), Fresh Raspberry Pie (p. 14), Raspberry Cream Tarts (p. 79)

185 FRESH-BAKED PLEASURES

Few things are more heartwarming or heavenly than a slice of pie. Whether the occasion is big or small, lavish or simple…a from-scratch pie will melt any and all resistance to dessert!

Featuring seasonal fruit-filled classics, silky cream creations, frosty indulgences and berry-laden tarts, cobblers and other tried-and-true favorites, *Taste of Home Best-Loved Pies* has all the right ingredients for creating flaky perfection.

When you crave a sweet something that bubbles warm and delicious with your favorite fruit, lattice-crowned delights such as ruby-red Fresh Cherry Pie (p. 13) and succulent Cranberry-Pecan Pear Pie (p. 26) are ripe-for-the-picking.

If your palate is pleased with pies of the soft, smooth and creamy variety, then you're sure to fall in love with dreamy classics such as Creamy Banana-Berry Pie (p. 39) or Caramel Chocolate Mousse Pie (p. 52).

Need to cool off on a hot summer afternoon? You can't go wrong with Frosty Key Lime Pie (p. 60), Frozen Grasshopper Torte (p. 72) or one of the many chilly treats *Best-Loved Pies* has to offer.

In addition to pies, this kitchen classic serves up tangy, fruit-filled tarts, yummy dessert pizzas and a host of cobblers, crumbles, crisps and other delights baked with old-fashioned goodness. And because a flaky, golden crust is the hallmark of a perfect pie, we've included handy pointers and recipes for homemade dough, so you can make foolproof, from-scratch pastry each and every time.

So go ahead…roll up your sleeves and pull out your rolling pin! With these luscious recipes, handy baking tips, easy-to-follow instructions and gorgeous full-color photos, *Best-Loved Pies* makes it as easy as pie to end dinner on a sweet note!

NO BAKE

Discover our wide assortment of "No-Bake" recipes! These are cool and quick desserts that don't require you to bake the filling. You'll find that they're ideal for busy weeknights or special events where time is of the essence. They're especially convenient in the summer when you don't want to turn on the oven, and kids can often help with these types of treats, too.

You may notice that some of these recipes require some initial baking time for the crust, whether it be a homemade pastry or frozen pie shell. They are still classified as "no-bake" because they do not set like traditional baked pies, which usually bake about an hour. If you like, you can replace many baked crusts with a pre-baked, store-bought crust, such as a graham cracker or chocolate crumb crust, saving you even more time. How sweet is that?

CONTENTS

PREPARING A CRUST
IS EASY AS
PIE

A GOLDEN HOMEMADE CRUST MADE UP OF THIN, CRISP LAYERS IS THE HALLMARK OF A PERFECT PIE. FLAKY CRUSTS LIKE THAT DELIVER SO MUCH APPEAL, IT'S HARD TO BELIEVE THEY HAVE JUST THREE BASIC COMPONENTS—FLOUR, FAT AND WATER. USE THE BASIC PIE PASTRY RECIPES AND TIPS ON THE FOLLOWING PAGES TO CREATE YOUR OWN PERFECT HOMEMADE CRUST. YOU'LL BE BLUE-RIBBON BOUND IN NO TIME!

PASTRY FOR SINGLE-CRUST PIE

PREP/TOTAL TIME: 30 MIN.

TASTE OF HOME TEST KITCHEN

1-1/4 cups all-purpose flour
1/2 teaspoon salt
1/3 cup shortening
4 to 5 tablespoons cold water

- In a bowl, combine flour and salt; cut in shortening until crumbly. Gradually add water, tossing with a fork until dough forms a ball. Roll out to fit a 9-in. pie plate. Transfer pastry to pie plate. Trim pastry to 1/2 in. beyond edge of plate; flute edges. Fill or bake according to recipe directions.

YIELD: 1 PASTRY SHELL (9 INCHES).

PASTRY FOR DOUBLE-CRUST PIE

PREP/TOTAL TIME: 20 MIN.

TASTE OF HOME TEST KITCHEN

2 cups all-purpose flour
3/4 teaspoon salt
2/3 cup shortening
6 to 7 tablespoons cold water

- In a bowl, combine flour and salt; cut in the shortening until crumbly. Gradually add the water, tossing with a fork until dough forms a ball. Divide dough in half so that one ball is slightly larger than the other. Roll out larger ball to fit a 9-in. pie plate. Transfer pastry to pie plate. Trim pastry even with edge. Pour desired filling into crust. Roll out second ball. Position over filling; cut slits in pastry. Trim pastry to 1 in. beyond edge of pie plate. Fold top crust over bottom crust. Flute edges. Bake according to recipe directions.

YIELD: 1 PASTRY SHELL (9 INCHES).

NEVER-FAIL PIE CRUST

PREP: 15 MIN. + CHILLING

RUTH GRITTER • GRAND RAPIDS, MICHIGAN

2 cups all-purpose flour
1 teaspoon salt
2/3 cup shortening
1/3 cup milk
1 tablespoon vinegar

- Combine flour and salt in a bowl. Cut in shortening. Add milk and vinegar. Shape dough into a ball. Chill for 30 minutes. Divide the dough in half. On a lightly floured surface, roll out each half to fit a 9-in. pie pan. Fill or bake according to recipe directions.

YIELD: 2 PASTRY SHELLS (9 INCHES).

PAT-IN-THE-PAN PIE CRUST

PREP: 10 MIN. BAKE: 10 MIN. + COOLING

MRS. ANTON SOHRWIEDE • MCGRAW, NEW YORK

1 cup all-purpose flour
1/3 cup sugar
1 teaspoon baking powder
1/4 teaspoon salt
2 tablespoons cold butter
1 egg, lightly beaten
2 tablespoons 2% milk

- In a large bowl, combine the flour, sugar, baking powder and salt; cut in butter until mixture resembles coarse crumbs. Combine egg and milk; stir into flour mixture (dough will be sticky). Press onto the bottom and up the sides of a greased 9-in. pie plate.

- Bake at 375° for 8-10 minutes or until set. Cool on a wire rack. Fill as desired.

  If baking the filling, cover edges with foil during the last 30 minutes to prevent overbrowning if necessary.

YIELD: 1 PIE CRUST (9 INCHES).

GRAHAM PIE CRUST MIX

PREP: 5 MIN. + CHILLING BAKE: 10 MIN.

SUE ROSS • CASA GRANDE, ARIZONA

5 cups graham cracker crumbs (about 40 squares)
1 cup sugar
1 cup cold butter, cubed
1 teaspoon ground cinnamon

- In a food processor, combine crumbs, sugar, butter and cinnamon; pulse until mixture becomes crumbly. Store in an airtight container in refrigerator for up to 3 months.

YIELD: ABOUT 7-1/2 CUPS MIX (ABOUT 4 PIE CRUSTS).

TO PREPARE ONE CRUST: Press about 1-3/4 cups crust mix onto the bottom and up the sides of a 9-in. pie plate. Bake at 375° for 8-10 minutes or until lightly browned. Chill 30 minutes before filling.

PIE PASTRY POINTERS

Whether you're a beginner or well-seasoned baker, you'll appreciate these practical pointers for creating homemade pastry for pies and tarts.

STARTING FROM SCRATCH

- Classic pie pastry recipes are prepared with solid shortening. Lard or butter-flavored shortening can be substituted for plain shortening if desired.

- Measure all ingredients accurately. Combine the flour and salt thoroughly before adding the shortening and water. Be sure to use ice-cold water. Add an ice cube to water and measure before adding it to the flour mixture.

- To produce a flaky crust, avoid overmixing when adding the water to the flour and shortening mixture. Overmixing develops gluten in the flour, causing the pastry to become tough.

- Chill pie pastry dough for 30 minutes before rolling to make it easier to handle.

- A floured surface is essential to prevent sticking when rolling out pastry. A pastry cloth and rolling pin cover are good investments—they will keep the pastry from sticking and minimize the amount of flour used. The less flour you add while rolling, the flakier and lighter the pie pastry will be.

- Choose dull-finish aluminum or glass pie plates for crisp, golden crusts. Shiny pans can produce soggy crusts. Because of the high-fat content in a pastry, do not grease the pie plate unless the recipe directs.

- Never prick the bottom of a pastry crust when the filling and crust are to be baked together.

- Use dried uncooked beans or rice atop heavy-duty foil to weigh down a crust when it's prebaked. The beans or rice prevent the sides of the pie crust from shrinking and slipping down the pie plate during baking. NOTE: Do not eat beans or rice.

TIPS FOR TASTIER CRUSTS

- To give a homemade pie crust a citrus twist, simply add a bit of grated orange or lemon peel to the flour mixture and use orange or lemon juice instead of water.

- For a sweeter crust, add a bit of confectioners' sugar or regular sugar along with a few drops of vanilla extract. Also sprinkle a bit of cinnamon or nutmeg over the pastry dough for apple or pumpkin pies.

- To give a crust a nutty taste, add a tablespoon of sesame seeds.

- For a firmer crust, add 1/8 teaspoon cream of tartar for every cup of flour.

MAKING CRUMB CRUSTS

Why rely on store-bought crumb crusts when you can easily prepare a better-tasting version from scratch?

Simply place cookies or crackers in a heavy-duty resealable plastic bag. Seal bag, pushing out as much air as possible. Press a rolling pin over the bag, crushing the crackers to fine crumbs. Crumbs can also be made in a blender or food processor according to the manufacturer's directions.

In a bowl, combine the crumbs, sugar and melted butter; blend well. Press the mixture onto the bottom and up the sides of an ungreased 9-in. pie plate. Chill 30 minutes before filling or bake at 375° for 8-10 minutes or until crust is lightly browned. Cool before filling.

TYPE OF CRUST	AMOUNT OF CRUMBS	SUGAR	BUTTER (MELTED)
Graham Cracker	1-1/2 cups (24 squares)	1/4 cup	1/3 cup
Chocolate Wafer	1-1/4 cups (20 wafers)	1/4 cup	1/4 cup
Vanilla Wafer	1-1/2 cups (30 wafers)	none	1/4 cup
Cream-Filled Chocolate	1-1/2 cups (15 cookies)	none	1/4 cup
Gingersnap	1-1/2 cups (24 cookies)	none	1/4 cup
Macaroon Cookie	1-1/2 cups	none	1/4 cup
Pretzel (grease pie pan)	1-1/4 cups	1/4 cup	1/2 cup

MAKING & SHAPING SINGLE- AND DOUBLE-CRUST PIE PASTRY

1 Accurately measure the flour and salt and combine in a bowl. Using a pastry blender or two knives, cut in the shortening until the mixture resembles course crumbs (the size of small peas).

2 Sprinkle 1 tablespoon of cold water over the mixture and toss gently with a fork. Repeat until the dry ingredients are moist and the dough holds together. Use only as much water as necessary.

3 Shape into a ball. (For a double-crust pie, divide pastry in half so that one ball is slightly larger than the other). On a floured surface or a floured pastry cloth, flatten the ball (the larger one if making a double-crust pie) into a neat circle, pressing together any cracks or breaks.

4 Roll the dough with a floured rolling pin from the center of the pastry to the edges, forming a circle 2 inches larger than the pie plate. The pastry should be about 1/8 inch thick.

5 To move pastry to the pie plate, roll up onto the rolling pin. Position over the edge of the pie plate and unroll. Let the pastry ease into the plate. Do not stretch the pastry to fit. For a single-crust pie, trim the pastry with kitchen scissors to 1/2 inch beyond the plate edge; turn under and flute as in step 8. Either bake the shell or fill according to the recipe's directions. For a double-crust pie, trim the pastry even with the edge of the plate. For a lattice-crust, trim pastry to 1 inch beyond the plate edge.

6 For a double-crust pie, roll out the second ball into a 12-inch circle, about 1/8 inch thick. Roll up pastry onto rolling pin; position over filling. With a knife, cut slits in top to allow steam to escape while baking.

7 With scissors, trim top pastry to 1 inch beyond the plate edge. Fold the top pastry over the bottom pastry.

8 To flute the edge, position your thumb on the inside of the crust. Place your thumb and index finger of your other hand on the outside edge and pinch pastry around your thumb to form a V-shape and seal the dough together. Continue around the edge. Bake according to recipe directions.

DECORATIVE PIE CRUSTS

A fold here, a twist there—with some simple but snappy finger work, you can turn out a pie or tart that's as yummy to look at as it is to eat.

Eye-catching edges, cutout pieces of pastry and well-woven lattice tops all give pie crusts fancy finishing touches. And although they may look difficult, you'll find these tasty decorations are a cinch to complete.

To help unravel the mystery behind making such appealing crusts, we've compiled simple-to-follow instructions on time-tested treatments, so you can create your own at home.

FLUTED EDGE CRUST

1 A fluted or ruffle edge is suitable for a single- or double-crust pie. Line a 9-in. pie plate with the bottom crust.

2 Trim the pastry to 1/2 in. beyond the rim of the pie plate for a single-crust pie and 1 in. for a double-crust pie. Then turn the overhang under to form the built-up edge.

3 Position your thumb and index finger about 1 in. apart on the edge of the crust, pointing out. Position the index finger on your other hand between the two fingers and gently push the pastry toward the center in an upward direction. Continue around the edge.

SCALLOPED EDGE CRUST

1 A cut scalloped edge is suitable for a single-crust pie. Line a 9-in. pie plate with the bottom crust and trim the pastry even with the edge of the plate.

2 Hold a teaspoon or tablespoon upside down and roll the tip of the spoon around the edge of the pastry to cut it. Remove and discard the cut pieces to create a scalloped pattern. Remember—the larger the spoon, the bigger the scallops.

ROPE EDGE CRUST

1 A rope edge is suitable for a single- or double-crust pie. Trim pastry to 1/2 in. beyond the rim of the pie plate for a single-crust pie and 1 in. for a double-crust pie. Then turn the overhang under to form the built-up edge.

2 Make a fist with one hand and press your thumb at an angle into the dough. Pinch some of the dough between your thumb and index finger.

3 Repeat at about 1/2-in. intervals around the crust. For a looser-looking rope, position your thumb at a wider angle and repeat at 1-in. intervals.

LEAF TRIM CRUST

1 A leaf trim is suitable for a single-crust pie. Make enough pastry for a double crust. Line a 9-in. pie plate with the bottom crust and trim the pastry even with the edge of the pie plate. Roll out the remaining dough to 1/8-in. thickness.

2 Cut out leaf shapes using 1-in. to 1-1/2-in. cookie cutters. With a sharp knife, score dough to create leaf vines. Brush bottom of each leaf with water.

3 Place one or two layers of leaves around the pasty edge. Press lightly to secure. Use foil to protect the edges from overbrowning. You can also use this technique with other cookie cutter designs, such as stars, hearts, apples or any shape of your choice. Vary them to suit the special occasion or season you are celebrating.

LATTICE TOP CRUST

1 A lattice top crust is suitable for a double-crust pie. Line bottom of a 9-in. pie plate with half the pastry and add the filling. Roll remaining dough into an 11-in. circle. Cut 1-in.-wide strips using a knife, pizza cutter or clean pinking shears for a scalloped edge. Lay half the strips across the pie, about 1 inch apart.

2 Fold back every other strip about halfway. Lay a strip of dough across center of pie at a right angle to the other strips. Unfold strips over the center strip.

3 Fold back the alternate strips; place second cross strip in place. Continue to add strips until the entire pie is covered with lattice.

4 Trim all but 1 in. of the overlapping dough; fold the edges under bottom crust. Pinch dough around edge of pie to form a decorative edge.

FINISHING TOUCHES FOR PIE CRUSTS

To top off double-crust pies before baking, use a pastry brush to lightly and evenly apply one of the following washes to the top crust, avoiding the edges.

- For a shine and light browning, brush with an egg white that was lightly beaten with 1 teaspoon of water.

- For a glossy, golden appearance, brush with an egg yolk that was beaten with 1 teaspoon of water.

- For a slight shine, brush with half-and-half cream or heavy whipping cream.

- For a crisp brown crust, brush with water.

- For a little sparkle, sprinkle with the sugar or decorator sugar after brushing with one of the washes.

- To give a little more shine to a baked double-crust pie, warm 1 tablespoon of light corn syrup. Gently brush over the baked warm crust.

FRUIT PIES & OTHER CLASSICS

LOOK NO FURTHER TO FIND A COLLECTION OF FRUITY SENSATIONS THAT BAKE TO FLAKY PERFECTION. THIS CHAPTER ALSO OFFERS A SWEET SELECTION OF CLASSIC NUT, PUMPKIN AND SWEET POTATO PIES.

FRESH RASPBERRY PIE

FLORIDA PIE

PREP: 25 MIN. **BAKE:** 15 MIN. + CHILLING

*I'm from the Midwest so I put winter in its place
with this light and lovely orange meringue pie
that tastes just as sun-kissed as it looks.*

MURIEL BOYD • ROSCOE, ILLINOIS

- 1 cup sugar
- 5 tablespoons cornstarch
- 1-1/2 cups orange juice
- 3 egg yolks, lightly beaten
- 2 large navel oranges, peeled, sectioned and finely chopped
- 2 tablespoons butter
- 1 tablespoon grated orange peel
- 1 tablespoon lemon juice
- 1 pastry shell (9 inches), baked

MERINGUE:

- 3 egg whites
- 2 tablespoons sugar

- In a small saucepan, combine the sugar and cornstarch. Stir in orange juice until smooth. Cook and stir over medium-high heat until thickened and bubbly. Reduce heat; cook and stir 2 minutes longer.

- Remove from the heat. Stir a small amount of hot filling into egg yolks; return all to the pan, stirring constantly. Bring to a gentle boil; cook and stir for 2 minutes. Remove from the heat. Stir in the oranges, butter and orange peel. Gently stir in the lemon juice. Pour into pastry shell.

- In a small bowl, beat the egg whites on medium speed until soft peaks form. Gradually add sugar, 1 teaspoon at a time, beating on high until stiff glossy peaks form and sugar is dissolved. Spread evenly over hot filling, sealing edges to crust.

- Bake at 350° for 15 minutes or until meringue is golden brown. Cool on a wire rack for 1 hour. Refrigerate for at least 3 hours before serving. Refrigerate leftovers.

YIELD: 8 SERVINGS.

CARAMEL NUT PIE

CARAMEL NUT PIE

PREP: 15 MIN. **BAKE:** 30 MIN. + CHILLING

*My clan loves this sweet-and-salty pie.
It tastes like a candy bar in a pie!*

DULCIE KNOLL • BLUFFTON, SOUTH CAROLINA

- 3 eggs
- 3/4 cup Milky Way ice cream topping
- 1/2 cup sugar
- 1/4 cup light corn syrup
- 2 tablespoons butter, melted
- 1 teaspoon vanilla extract
- 1/8 teaspoon salt
- 1 unbaked pastry shell (9 inches)
- 1 cup chopped unsalted dry roasted peanuts
- 1/2 cup chopped walnuts

- In a small bowl, whisk the eggs, ice cream topping, sugar, corn syrup, butter, vanilla and salt until blended. Pour into pastry shell; sprinkle with nuts. Cover edges with foil.

- Bake at 400° for 10 minutes. Reduce heat to 350°; bake 20-25 minutes longer or until filling is almost set. Cool on a wire rack. Refrigerate for 1-2 hours before serving.

YIELD: 6-8 SERVINGS.

FLORIDA PIE

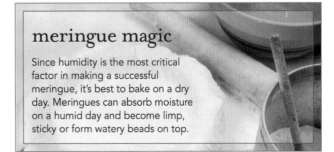

meringue magic

Since humidity is the most critical factor in making a successful meringue, it's best to bake on a dry day. Meringues can absorb moisture on a humid day and become limp, sticky or form watery beads on top.

SWEET POTATO PIE

SWEET POTATO PIE
PREP: 25 MIN. BAKE: 45 MIN. + COOLING

I rely on this simple but special deep-dish pie to provide a down-home finish to hearty autumn meals. Pecans and pumpkin pie spice make this a comforting, seasonal classic.

PAUL AZZONE • SHOREHAM, NEW YORK

- 1-2/3 cups pie crust mix
- 1/4 cup chopped pecans
- 3 to 4 tablespoons cold water
- 3 eggs
- 2 cans (15 ounces each) sweet potatoes, drained
- 1 can (14 ounces) sweetened condensed milk
- 1-1/2 to 2 teaspoons pumpkin pie spice
- 1 teaspoon vanilla extract
- 1/2 teaspoon salt

Whipped topping and additional chopped pecans, toasted, optional

- In a small bowl, combine the pie crust mix and pecans. Gradually add water, tossing with a fork until dough forms a ball. Roll out to fit a 9-in. deep-dish pie plate. Transfer pastry to pie plate. Flute edges; set aside.

- In a food processor, combine the eggs, sweet potatoes, milk, pumpkin pie spice, vanilla and salt; blend until smooth. Pour into pastry.

- Bake at 425° for 15 minutes. Reduce heat to 350°; bake 30-35 minutes longer or until a knife inserted near the center comes out clean. Cool on a wire rack. Garnish with whipped topping and toasted pecans if desired.

YIELD: 8 SERVINGS.

BEST LEMON MERINGUE PIE
PREP: 45 MIN. BAKE: 10 MIN. + CHILLING

Here's a tart and tangy, tiny-enough-for-two pie that's proof good things still come in small packages!

SHERIE SNITKER • WICHITA, KANSAS

- 1/2 cup all-purpose flour
- 1/8 teaspoon salt
- 2 tablespoons shortening
- 2 tablespoons water

FILLING:
- 1/2 cup sugar
- 2 tablespoons cornstarch
- 1/8 teaspoon salt
- 1/2 cup water
- 2 egg yolks, beaten
- 2 teaspoons butter
- 2 tablespoons lemon juice
- 1/4 teaspoon grated lemon peel

MERINGUE:
- 1 egg white
- 1/4 teaspoon lemon juice
- 1 tablespoon sugar

- In a small bowl, combine the flour and salt; cut in the shortening until mixture is crumbly. Gradually add the water, tossing with a fork until a ball forms. Cover and refrigerate for 15 minutes or until easy to handle.

- On a lightly floured surface, roll out pastry to fit a 5-in. pie plate. Transfer pastry to pie plate; trim to 1/2 in. beyond edge of plate. Flute edges. Line unpricked pastry shell with a double thickness of heavy-duty foil. Bake at 450° for 5 minutes. Remove foil; bake 5 minutes longer. Cool on a wire rack.

- For filling, in a small saucepan, combine the sugar, cornstarch and salt. Gradually stir in water until smooth. Cook and stir over medium heat until thickened and bubbly. Reduce heat; cook and stir 2 minutes longer. Remove from the heat. Gradually stir 2 tablespoons hot

BEST LEMON MERINGUE PIE

TEXAS PECAN PIE

filling into egg yolks; return all to the pan, stirring constantly. Bring to a gentle boil; cook and stir 2 minutes longer. Remove from the heat. Gently stir in butter, lemon juice and peel. Pour into crust.

- For meringue, in a small bowl, beat egg white and lemon juice on medium speed until soft peaks form. Gradually beat in sugar on high until stiff glossy peaks form and sugar is dissolved. Spread evenly over hot filling, sealing edges to crust.

- Bake at 350° for 10-12 minutes or until the meringue is golden. Cool on a wire rack for 30 minutes. Refrigerate for at least 3 hours before serving.

YIELD: 2 SERVINGS.

TEXAS PECAN PIE
PREP: 20 MIN. BAKE: 1 HOUR + COOLING

This ooey, gooey pie's luscious and creamy filling offers that good old familiar flavor so many have come to love!

LAUREL LESLIE • SONORA, CALIFORNIA

1/2	cup sugar
3	tablespoons all-purpose flour
1	cup light corn syrup
1	cup dark corn syrup
3	eggs
1	teaspoon white vinegar
1/2	teaspoon vanilla extract
1	cup chopped pecans

Pastry for single-crust pie (9 inches)

- In a large bowl, whisk the sugar, flour, corn syrups, eggs, vinegar and vanilla until smooth. Stir in pecans. Pour into pastry shell. Cover edges with foil.

- Bake at 350° for 35 minutes. Remove foil; bake 25-30 minutes longer or until a knife inserted near the center comes out clean. Cool on a wire rack. Refrigerate any leftovers.

YIELD: 8 SERVINGS.

FRESH CHERRY PIE
PREP: 25 MIN. BAKE: 55 MIN. + COOLING

This ruby-red treat is just sweet enough, with a hint of almond flavor and a good level of cinnamon. The cherries peeking out of the lattice crust make it so pretty, too.

JOSIE BOCHEK • STURGEON BAY, WISCONSIN

1-1/4	cups sugar
1/3	cup cornstarch
1	cup cherry juice blend
4	cups fresh tart cherries, pitted or frozen pitted tart cherries, thawed
1/2	teaspoon ground cinnamon
1/4	teaspoon ground nutmeg
1/4	teaspoon almond extract

PASTRY:

2	cups all-purpose flour
1/2	teaspoon salt
2/3	cup shortening
3	to 4 tablespoons cold water

- In a large saucepan, combine sugar and cornstarch; gradually stir in cherry juice until smooth. Bring to a boil; cook and stir for 2 minutes or until thickened. Remove from the heat. Add the cherries, cinnamon, nutmeg and extract; set aside.

- In a large bowl, combine the flour and salt; cut in the shortening until crumbly. Gradually add cold water, tossing with a fork until a ball forms. Divide pastry in half so that one ball is slightly larger than the other.

- On a lightly floured surface, roll out larger ball to fit a 9-in. pie plate. Transfer pastry to pie plate; trim even with edge of plate. Add filling. Roll out remaining pastry; make a lattice crust. Trim, seal and flute edges.

- Bake at 425° for 10 minutes. Reduce heat to 375°; bake 45-50 minutes longer or until crust is golden brown. Cool on a wire rack.

YIELD: 8 SERVINGS.

FRESH CHERRY PIE

FRESH RASPBERRY PIE

PREP: 35 MIN. + CHILLING BAKE: 50 MIN. + COOLING

A slice of this raspberry gem was practically a staple at our house during the late summer. Our family had raspberry bushes, so the pie was always made with fresh-picked berries.

EMILY DENNIS • HANCOCK, MICHIGAN

- 2 cups all-purpose flour
- 1 tablespoon sugar
- 1/2 teaspoon salt
- 3/4 cup shortening
- 1 egg, lightly beaten
- 3 tablespoons cold water
- 1 tablespoon white vinegar

FILLING:
- 1-1/3 cups sugar
- 2 tablespoons quick-cooking tapioca
- 2 tablespoons cornstarch
- 5 cups fresh or frozen unsweetened raspberries, thawed
- 1 tablespoon butter

TOPPING:
- 1 tablespoon 2% milk
- 1 tablespoon sugar

- In a large bowl, combine the flour, sugar and salt; cut in shortening until the mixture resembles coarse crumbs. Combine egg, water and vinegar; stir into flour mixture just until moistened. Divide dough in half so that one ball is slightly larger than the other; wrap each in plastic wrap. Refrigerate for 30 minutes or until easy to handle.

- In another large bowl, combine the sugar, tapioca, cornstarch and raspberries; let stand for 15 minutes.

- On a lightly floured surface, roll out larger ball of dough to fit a 9-in. pie plate. Transfer dough to pie plate; trim even with edge. Add raspberry filling; dot with butter.

FRESH RASPBERRY PIE

LEMON MERINGUE PIE

- Roll out remaining dough to fit top of pie; place over filling. Trim, seal and flute edges. Cut slits in top. Brush with milk; sprinkle with sugar.

- Bake at 350° for 50-55 minutes or until crust is golden brown and filling is bubbly. Cool on a wire rack.

YIELD: 6-8 SERVINGS.

LEMON MERINGUE PIE

PREP: 35 MIN. BAKE: 15 MIN. + CHILLING

My grandmother gave me the recipe for this classic lemon delight. Not only does it taste divine, it evokes memories of her warmth and the comfort of home.

MERLE DYCK • ELKFORD, BRITISH COLUMBIA

- 1/2 cup sugar
- 1/4 cup cornstarch

Pinch salt
- 2 cups cold water
- 2 egg yolks, lightly beaten
- 3 tablespoons lemon juice
- 1 teaspoon grated lemon peel
- 1 teaspoon butter

MERINGUE:
- 3 egg whites
- 1/8 teaspoon cream of tartar
- 6 tablespoons sugar

Pastry for single-crust pie (9 inches), baked

- In a large saucepan, combine the sugar, cornstarch and salt. Stir in water until smooth. Cook and stir over medium heat until thickened and bubbly, about 2 minutes. Reduce heat; cook and stir 2 minutes longer.

- Remove from the heat. Gradually stir 1 cup hot filling into egg yolks; return all to the pan. Bring to a gentle boil; cook and stir for 2 minutes. Remove from the heat. Gently stir in lemon juice, peel and butter until butter is melted. Set aside and keep warm.

- For meringue, in a small bowl, beat egg whites and cream of tartar on medium speed until soft peaks form. Gradually beat in sugar, 1 tablespoon at a time, on high until stiff glossy peaks form and sugar is dissolved.

- Pour filling into crust. Spread meringue over hot filling, sealing edges to crust. Bake at 350° for 15 minutes or until meringue is golden brown. Cool on a wire rack for 1 hour; refrigerate for at least 3 hours before serving.

YIELD: 8 SERVINGS.

CRANBERRY PEAR CRISP PIE
PREP: 25 MIN. BAKE: 55 MIN. + COOLING

Filled with a bubbling combination of cranberries and pears, this crumb-topped dessert is a wonderful change of pace from traditional fruit pies.

PRISCILLA GILBERT • INDIAN HARBOUR BEACH, FLORIDA

5	cups sliced peeled fresh pears
1	tablespoon lemon juice
1	teaspoon vanilla extract
1-2/3	cups fresh or frozen cranberries
1/2	cup packed brown sugar
1/3	cup all-purpose flour
1	unbaked pastry shell (9 inches)

TOPPING:
1/4	cup all-purpose flour
1/4	cup quick-cooking oats
3	tablespoons packed brown sugar
3/4	teaspoon ground cinnamon
2	tablespoons cold butter

CRANBERRY PEAR CRISP PIE

CINNAMON PUMPKIN PIE

- Place the pears in a large bowl; sprinkle with lemon juice and vanilla. Add cranberries. Combine the brown sugar and flour; sprinkle over fruit and gently toss to coat. Spoon into pastry shell.

- In a small bowl, combine the flour, oats, brown sugar and cinnamon. Cut in the butter until crumbly. Sprinkle the topping over filling.

- Cover edges of pastry loosely with foil. Bake at 375° for 30 minutes. Remove foil; bake 25-30 minutes longer or until filling is bubbly. Cool on a wire rack.

YIELD: 8 SERVINGS.

CINNAMON PUMPKIN PIE
PREP: 10 MIN. BAKE: 55 MIN. + COOLING

This recipe is a breeze to make and tastes delicious. It's a top request for family gatherings.

JACQUELINE DEIBERT • KLINGERSTOWN, PENNSYLVANIA

1	cup sugar
4	teaspoons cornstarch
1/2	teaspoon salt
1/2	teaspoon ground cinnamon
2	eggs
1	can (15 ounces) solid-pack pumpkin
1	cup milk
1	unbaked pastry shell (9 inches)

Whipped cream in a can, optional

- In a small bowl, combine the sugar, cornstarch, salt and cinnamon. In a large bowl, beat eggs. Stir in pumpkin and sugar mixture. Gradually stir in the milk. Pour into pastry shell.

- Bake at 400° for 10 minutes. Reduce heat to 350°; bake 45-50 minutes longer or until a knife inserted near the center comes out clean. Cool on a wire rack. Top with whipped cream if desired. Refrigerate leftovers.

YIELD: 6 SERVINGS.

MAKEOVER SWEET POTATO PECAN PIE

MAKEOVER SWEET POTATO PECAN PIE
PREP: 25 MIN. BAKE: 45 MIN. + CHILLING

This recipe makeover was a giant success. The original, a marvel on its own, was transformed into a richer, better-for-you pie with even more fall spices. It's delicious for the holidays or anytime you want a light dessert.

MARGIE WILLIAMS • MT. JULIET, TENNESSEE

1	sheet refrigerated pie pastry
1-1/2	cups mashed sweet potatoes
1/3	cup 2% milk
1/4	cup packed dark brown sugar
1	tablespoon reduced-fat butter, melted
1/2	teaspoon vanilla extract
1/4	teaspoon salt
1/2	teaspoon ground cinnamon
1/4	teaspoon ground allspice
1/4	teaspoon ground nutmeg

PECAN LAYER:

1	egg
1/3	cup packed dark brown sugar
1/3	cup corn syrup
1	tablespoon reduced-fat butter, melted
1/4	teaspoon vanilla extract
2/3	cup chopped pecans

- On a lightly floured surface, unroll pastry. Transfer to a 9-in. pie plate. Trim pastry to 1/2 in. beyond edge of plate; flute edges.

- In a small bowl, combine sweet potatoes, milk, brown sugar, butter, vanilla, salt and spices. Spread evenly into pastry shell.

- For pecan layer, in another small bowl, whisk egg and brown sugar until blended. Add the corn syrup, butter

and vanilla; mix well. Stir in pecans. Pour over sweet potato mixture.

- Bake at 350° for 45-55 minutes or until a knife inserted near the center comes out clean. Cool completely on a wire rack. Refrigerate pie for at least 3 hours before serving.

YIELD: 8 SERVINGS.

EDITOR'S NOTE: This recipe was tested with Land O'Lakes light stick butter.

WALNUT MOLASSES PIE
PREP: 10 MIN. + CHILLING BAKE: 40 MIN. + COOLING

This pie is a family favorite I frequently prepare for Sunday dinner at my mom's house. Somewhat like pecan pie, this treat is scrumptious and nutty with a sweet molasses flavor.

BETTY JONES • COLLINSTON, LOUISIANA

3	eggs
3/4	cup light corn syrup
2/3	cup sugar
1/3	cup butter, melted
1/4	cup molasses
1	teaspoon vanilla extract
1-1/2	cups chopped walnuts
1	unbaked pastry shell (9 inches)

- In a bowl, whisk the eggs, corn syrup, sugar, butter, molasses and vanilla until blended; stir in walnuts. Pour into pastry shell. Cover edges with foil.

- Bake at 350° for 25 minutes; remove foil. Bake 12-17 minutes longer or until top of pie is set and crust is golden brown. Cool on a wire rack. Refrigerate for 1-2 hours before cutting.

YIELD: 6-8 SERVINGS.

RHUBARB RUMBLE
PREP: 30 MIN. + CHILLING

(NO BAKE)

I first tried this at a potluck and immediately asked for the recipe. I was pleased to discover it was sugar-free.

CHARLA SACKMANN • GLIDDEN, IOWA

3	cups chopped rhubarb
1	package (.3 ounce) sugar-free strawberry gelatin
1-1/2	cups cold skim milk
1	package (1 ounce) instant sugar-free vanilla pudding mix
1	reduced-fat graham cracker crust (8 inches)

- Place the rhubarb in a microwave-safe bowl; cover and microwave on high for 6-8 minutes or until rhubarb is softened, stirring every 2 minutes. Stir in the gelatin until dissolved; cool completely.

- In a bowl, combine milk and pudding mix; beat on low speed for 2 minutes. Fold into rhubarb mixture. Spoon into crust. Cover and refrigerate until firm.

YIELD: 8 SERVINGS.

EDITOR'S NOTE: This recipe was tested in a 1,100-watt microwave.

CHERRY-APPLE LATTICE PIE
PREP: 20 MIN. BAKE: 45 MIN. + COOLING

This fruity sensation is one of my family's favorite desserts. At harvesttime or any time, it can't be beat!

LEANN SAGER • FAIRMONT, MINNESOTA

1/2	cup dried cherries
1/4	cup unsweetened apple juice
2	tablespoons plus 1/2 cup sugar, divided
2-1/4	teaspoons ground cinnamon, divided
2	tablespoons cornstarch
6	cups thinly sliced peeled tart apples
1	teaspoon vanilla extract
1	package (15 ounces) refrigerated pie pastry
1	egg white

- In a small microwave-safe bowl, combine cherries and apple juice. Cover and microwave on high until heated through; set aside.

- In a small bowl, combine 2 tablespoons sugar and 1/4 teaspoon cinnamon; set aside for topping. In a large bowl, combine the cornstarch with the remaining sugar and cinnamon. Stir in the apples, vanilla and reserved cherry mixture.

- Line a 9-in. deep-dish pie plate with bottom crust; trim pastry even with edge of plate. Add the filling. With remaining pastry, make a lattice crust. Seal and flute edges. Beat egg white until foamy; brush over lattice top. Sprinkle with reserved cinnamon-sugar.

- Cover edges loosely with foil. Bake at 450° for 15 minutes. Reduce heat to 350° and remove foil. Bake 30-45 minutes longer or until crust is golden brown and filling is bubbly. Cool on a wire rack.

YIELD: 8 SERVINGS.

SPICED PLUM PIE
PREP: 20 MIN. BAKE: 45 MIN. + COOLING

The subtle tastes of orange and nutmeg bring out the fresh flavor of plums in this comforting pie. Be sure to have a slice while it's still warm with a scoop of vanilla ice cream.

LUCILLE MEAD • ILION, NEW YORK

	Pastry for double-crust pie (9 inches)
4-1/2	cups sliced fresh plums
2/3	cup sugar
1/4	cup all-purpose flour
1	teaspoon ground cinnamon
1/4	teaspoon salt
1/4	teaspoon ground nutmeg
1	egg, lightly beaten
1/2	cup orange juice
1	teaspoon grated orange peel
2	tablespoons butter
	Vanilla ice cream, optional

- Line a 9-in. pie plate with bottom pastry; trim even with edge. Arrange plums in crust. In a small bowl, combine the sugar, flour, cinnamon, salt and nutmeg. Stir in the egg, orange juice and peel. Pour over plums and dot with butter.

- Roll out remaining pastry to fit top of pie; place over filling. Trim, seal and flute edges. Cut slits in pastry.

- Bake at 400° for 45-50 minutes or until crust is golden brown and filling is bubbly (cover the edges with foil during the last 15 minutes to prevent overbrowning if necessary). Cool on a wire rack for 10 minutes before cutting. Serve warm with ice cream if desired.

YIELD: 8 SERVINGS.

SPICED PLUM PIE

CARAMEL-PECAN CHEESECAKE PIE

PREP: 15 MIN. BAKE: 35 MIN. + CHILLING

In fall or any time of year, this nutty, rich and delicious pie is one I am proud to serve. It looks so impressive that folks are surprised to find it's so easy to make.

BECKY RUFF • MONONA, IOWA

1	sheet refrigerated pie pastry
1	package (8 ounces) cream cheese, softened
1/2	cup sugar
4	eggs
1	teaspoon vanilla extract
1-1/4	cups chopped pecans
1	jar (12-1/4 ounces) fat-free caramel ice cream topping

- Line a 9-in. pie plate with pastry. Trim and flute edges. In a small bowl, beat the cream cheese, sugar, 1 egg and vanilla until smooth. Spread into pastry shell; sprinkle with pecans.

- In a small bowl, whisk remaining eggs; gradually whisk in caramel topping until blended. Pour slowly over pecans.

- Bake at 375° for 35-40 minutes or until lightly browned (loosely cover edges with foil after 20 minutes if pie browns too quickly). Cool on a wire rack for 1 hour. Refrigerate for 4 hours or overnight before slicing.

YIELD: 6-8 SERVINGS.

EDITOR'S NOTE: This recipe was tested with Smucker's ice cream topping.

CARAMEL-PECAN CHEESECAKE PIE

CLASSIC PUMPKIN PIE

CLASSIC PUMPKIN PIE

PREP: 20 MIN. BAKE: 45 MIN. + COOLING

You can savor every delectable bite of this traditional treat topped with a crown of golden pastry "leaves."

TASTE OF HOME TEST KITCHEN

1	cup all-purpose flour
1	teaspoon sugar
1/4	teaspoon salt
3	tablespoons canola oil
1	tablespoon butter, melted
2	to 3 tablespoons cold water

FILLING:

1	egg
1	egg white
1/2	cup packed brown sugar
1/4	cup sugar
1/2	teaspoon salt
1/2	teaspoon ground cinnamon
1/8	teaspoon each ground allspice, nutmeg and cloves
1	can (15 ounces) solid-pack pumpkin
1	cup fat-free evaporated milk

- In a small bowl, combine the flour, sugar and salt. Using a fork, stir in oil and butter until dough is crumbly. Gradually add enough water until dough holds together. Roll out between sheets of plastic wrap into an 11-in. circle. Freeze for 10 minutes.

- Remove top sheet of plastic wrap; invert pastry into a 9-in. pie plate. Remove remaining plastic wrap. Trim and flute edges. Chill.

- Roll pastry scraps to 1/8-in. thickness. Cut with a 1-in. leaf-shaped cookie cutter. Place on an ungreased baking sheet. Bake at 375° for 6-8 minutes or until edges are very lightly browned. Cool on a wire rack.

- In a large bowl, beat the egg, egg white, sugars, salt and spices until smooth. Beat in the pumpkin. Gradually beat in the milk. Pour into the pastry shell. Bake at 375° for 45-50 minutes or until a knife inserted near the center comes out clean. Cool on a wire rack. Garnish with leaf cutouts. Refrigerate leftovers.

YIELD: 8 SERVINGS.

CONCORD GRAPE PIE
PREP: 35 MIN. BAKE: 25 MIN. + COOLING

Who would have thought grapes could make such a wonderful pie filling? The pleasing fruit lends a unique flavor sensation that will tingle your taste buds.

THOM BORCHERT • BELLA VISTA, ARKANSAS

3	cups Concord grapes
1	cup plus 1 teaspoon sugar, divided
3	tablespoons all-purpose flour
1	tablespoon sour cream
1/2	teaspoon lemon juice
1/8	teaspoon salt

Pastry for a double-crust pie (9 inches)
1   egg yolk, lightly beaten

- Remove skins from grapes by pinching grapes at end opposite stem (pulp pops out); reserve skins. In a saucepan, simmer pulp for 6 minutes or until seeds are loosened, stirring constantly. Press pulp through a sieve; discard seeds.

- In a saucepan, combine the pulp and reserved grape skins. Combine 1 cup sugar and flour; stir into sour cream. Add the sour cream mixture, lemon juice and salt to grape mixture. Bring to a boil; cook and stir for 2 minutes. Remove from heat.

- Line a 9-in. pie plate with bottom crust; trim pastry and flute edge. Pour filling into crust. Roll out the remaining pastry and cut out a 6-in. circle. Center circle over pie filling. (Discard remaining pastry or save for another use.) Brush circle with egg yolk; sprinkle with the remaining sugar. Bake at 400° for 25-30 minutes or until golden brown. Cool on a wire rack. Store in the refrigerator.

YIELD: 6-8 SERVINGS.

think thickeners

Thickeners help prevent fruit pies from being too runny. All-purpose flour, cornstarch and quick-cooking tapioca are the most common. They make slicing easy and keep the filling from bubbling over while baking.

STONE FRUIT PIE

STONE FRUIT PIE
PREP: 30 MIN. BAKE: 45 MIN.

You can use any type of stone fruit in this pie. My favorite combination is white peaches with tart cherries!

CRYSTAL JO BRUNS • ILIFF, COLORADO

2	cups fresh or frozen pitted tart cherries, thawed
3	medium nectarines, chopped
3	apricots, sliced
2/3	cup sugar
1	tablespoon cornstarch
2	tablespoons plus 2 cups all-purpose flour, divided
1/8	teaspoon ground cinnamon
1	teaspoon salt
3/4	cup plus 2 tablespoons cold butter, divided
6	to 7 tablespoons ice water
1	egg yolk
1	teaspoon water

- In a small bowl, combine the cherries, nectarines, apricots, sugar, cornstarch, 2 tablespoons flour and cinnamon; set aside.

- In another bowl, combine salt and remaining flour; cut in 3/4 cup butter until crumbly. Gradually add ice water, tossing with a fork until dough forms a ball. Divide dough in half. Roll out one half to fit a 9-in. pie plate; transfer pastry to pie plate. Add filling; dot with remaining butter.

- Roll out remaining pastry; make a lattice crust. Trim, seal and flute edges. In a small bowl, whisk the egg yolk and water; brush over lattice top. Bake at 400° for 45-50 minutes or until filling is bubbly and the crust is golden brown. Cover edges with foil during the last 15 minutes to prevent overbrowning if necessary. Cool on a wire rack.

YIELD: 8 SERVINGS.

GREEK HONEY NUT PIE
PREP: 30 MIN. BAKE: 40 MIN. + COOLING

I love Greek pastry, so I decided to combine phyllo dough, honey and walnuts to make a pie. The result was pure heaven.

ROSALIND JACKSON • STUART, FLORIDA

- 4 cups chopped walnuts
- 1/4 cup packed brown sugar
- 1 teaspoon ground cinnamon
- 1 package (16 ounces, 14-inch x 9-inch sheet size) frozen phyllo dough, thawed
- 1 cup butter, melted

SYRUP:
- 3/4 cup sugar
- 1/2 cup water
- 1/2 cup honey
- 1 teaspoon vanilla extract

Confectioners' sugar, lemon peel strips and additional honey

- In a large bowl, combine the walnuts, brown sugar and cinnamon; set aside.
- Place a sheet of phyllo dough in a greased 9-in. pie plate; brush with butter. (Keep remaining phyllo covered with plastic wrap and a damp towel to prevent it from drying out.) Repeat seven times. Sprinkle 1-1/3 cups nut mixture into crust.
- Place a sheet of phyllo over nut mixture; brush with butter. Repeat three times. Sprinkle with 1-1/3 cups nut mixture. Layer with another sheet of phyllo; brush with butter. Repeat three times. Sprinkle with the remaining nut mixture.
- Top with a sheet of phyllo; brush with the butter. Repeat seven times. Fold ends up onto top of pie; brush with the butter.

- Using a sharp knife, score pie into eight pieces. Cut a remaining phyllo sheet into thin strips and roll into rose shapes; arrange on top. Save remaining phyllo dough for another use.
- Bake at 350° for 40-45 minutes or until golden brown. Meanwhile, in a saucepan, combine the sugar, water and honey; bring to a boil. Reduce heat; simmer, uncovered, for 10 minutes. Add vanilla. Pour over warm pie. Cool on a wire rack. Garnish with confectioners' sugar, lemon peel and additional honey. Refrigerate leftovers.

YIELD: 8 SERVINGS.

GINGER PEAR PIE
PREP: 25 MIN. BAKE: 55 MIN.

This recipe comes from my grandmother, who yields a big harvest of pears from the trees on her land. A gingersnap crust complements the pleasant taste of the fruit.

MILDRED SHERRER • FORT WORTH, TEXAS

- 1 unbaked pastry shell (9 inches)
- 1/2 cup gingersnap crumbs (about 9 cookies)
- 1/4 cup sugar
- 1/4 cup packed brown sugar
- 1 tablespoon all-purpose flour
- 1/2 teaspoon salt
- 1/2 teaspoon ground cinnamon
- 1/4 cup cold butter, cubed
- 5 cups thinly sliced peeled pears (about 5 medium)

- Line unpricked pastry shell with a double thickness of heavy-duty foil. Bake at 450° for 8 minutes. Remove foil; bake 5 minutes longer. Cool on a wire rack.
- In a large bowl, combine the gingersnap crumbs, sugars, flour, salt and cinnamon. Cut in butter until crumbly. Place half the pear slices in crust. Top with half the crumb mixture. Repeat layers.
- Bake at 350° for 55-60 minutes or until golden. Cool on a wire rack. Cover edges with foil during the last 30 minutes to prevent overbrowning if necessary. Store in the refrigerator.

YIELD: 6-8 SERVINGS.

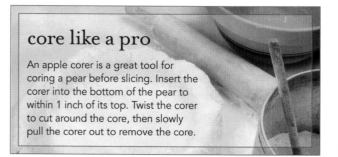

core like a pro

An apple corer is a great tool for coring a pear before slicing. Insert the corer into the bottom of the pear to within 1 inch of its top. Twist the corer to cut around the core, then slowly pull the corer out to remove the core.

FESTIVE PECAN PIE

FESTIVE PECAN PIE
PREP: 20 MIN. BAKE: 45 MIN.

The flavor of sweet pecans makes this dinner finale a winner every time. Folks ooh and ahh when they take their first bite.

PATTI ASTLE • BARABOO, WISCONSIN

1	sheet refrigerated pie pastry
1	egg, lightly beaten
2	tablespoons beaten egg
1/2	cup dark corn syrup
1/4	cup sugar
5	teaspoons butter
1/8	teaspoon salt
1/2	cup pecan halves

- Cut pastry sheet in half. Repackage and refrigerate one half for another use. On a lightly floured surface, roll out remaining half into an 8-in. circle. Transfer to a 7-in. pie plate; flute edges.

- In a small bowl, combine the next six ingredients until well mixed. Stir in the pecans. Pour into pie shell. Cover edges loosely with foil. Bake at 350° for 25 minutes. Remove foil; bake 20-25 minutes longer or until a knife inserted near the center comes out clean. Refrigerate any leftovers.

YIELD: 4 SERVINGS.

CRUMB-TOPPED APPLE & PUMPKIN PIE
PREP: 35 MIN. BAKE: 50 MIN. + COOLING

This special recipe combines all the warm, delicious flavors of autumn and makes a truly unique presentation. It gets rave reviews and has become a holiday tradition at our house.

TRISHA FOX • PLAINFIELD, ILLINOIS

1	sheet refrigerated pie pastry
2	cups thinly sliced peeled tart apples
1/4	cup sugar
2	teaspoons all-purpose flour
1	teaspoon lemon juice
1/4	teaspoon ground cinnamon

PUMPKIN FILLING:

1-1/2	cups canned pumpkin
1	cup fat-free evaporated milk
1/2	cup egg substitute
1/2	cup sugar
3/4	teaspoon ground cinnamon
1/4	teaspoon salt
1/8	teaspoon ground nutmeg

TOPPING:

1/2	cup all-purpose flour
3	tablespoons sugar
4-1/2	teaspoons cold butter
3	tablespoons chopped walnuts

- On a lightly floured surface, unroll pastry. Transfer the pastry to a 9-in. deep-dish pie plate. Trim the pastry to 1/2 in. beyond edge of plate; flute edges. In a large bowl, combine the apples, sugar, flour, lemon juice and cinnamon. Spoon into crust.

- In another large bowl, whisk pumpkin filling ingredients. Pour over apple mixture. Bake at 375° for 30 minutes.

- For topping, combine the flour and sugar. Cut in butter until crumbly; stir in walnuts. Sprinkle over pie.

- Bake 20-25 minutes longer or until a knife inserted into pumpkin layer comes out clean (cover edges with foil during the last 15 minutes to prevent overbrowning if necessary).

- Cool on a wire rack. Refrigerate leftovers.

YIELD: 10 SERVINGS.

CRUMB-TOPPED APPLE & PUMPKIN PIE

DEEP-DISH APPLE PIE

PREP: 50 MIN. **BAKE:** 40 MIN. + COOLING

*The delightful crust is filled deep with juicy apple slices.
Try this recipe for pie that is sure to be a winner.*

SALEM CROSS INN • WEST BROOKFIELD, MASSACHUSETTS

     2   cups all-purpose flour
   1/2   cup shortening
     1   egg
   1/4   cup cold water
     2   tablespoons white vinegar
FILLING:
    10   cups sliced peeled tart apples
     1   teaspoon lemon juice
   1/4   cup sugar
   1/4   cup packed brown sugar
     3   tablespoons all-purpose flour
     1   teaspoon ground cinnamon
   1/2   teaspoon ground nutmeg
     1   tablespoon butter
     1   egg
     1   tablespoon milk

- Place flour in a large bowl; cut in shortening until mixture resembles coarse crumbs. In a small bowl, combine the egg, water and vinegar; gradually add to the crumb mixture, tossing with a fork until a ball forms. Cover and refrigerate for 20 minutes or until easy to handle.

- Meanwhile, in a large bowl, toss apples with lemon juice. In a small bowl, combine the sugars, flour, cinnamon and nutmeg; add to apple mixture and toss to coat. Pour into a 13-in. x 9-in. baking dish; dot with butter.

- Roll out dough to fit top of pie. Flute edges. Beat egg with milk; brush over pastry. Bake at 375° for 40-50 minutes or until crust is golden brown and apples are tender. Cool on a wire rack.

YIELD: 15 SERVINGS.

DOUBLE-CRUST PEAR PIE

DOUBLE-CRUST PEAR PIE

PREP: 20 MIN. **BAKE:** 40 MIN. + COOLING

*This luscious pear pie bakes to flaky perfection and
is a nice change of pace from traditional apple pie.*

FAYE CREECH • MOORE, OKLAHOMA

   2/3   cup sugar
   1/4   cup cornstarch
     2   teaspoons grated lemon peel
 1-1/2   teaspoons crushed aniseed
 1-1/2   teaspoons lemon juice
     5   cups thinly sliced peeled ripe pears (about
         5 medium)
Pastry for double-crust pie (9 inches)
GLAZE:
   1/2   cup confectioners' sugar
     2   to 3 teaspoons lemon juice

- In a large bowl, combine the sugar, cornstarch, lemon peel, aniseed and lemon juice. Add the pears and toss gently.

- Line a 9-in. pie plate with bottom pastry; trim even with edge of plate. Add filling. Roll out remaining pastry to fit top of pie; place over filling. Trim, seal and flute edges. Cut slits in top.

- Bake at 400° for 40-45 minutes or until filling is bubbly and pears are tender. Cover the edges with foil during the last 20 minutes to prevent overbrowning. Combine glaze ingredients; gently spread over the hot pie. Cool completely on a wire rack. Store in the refrigerator.

YIELD: 6-8 SERVINGS.

DEEP-DISH APPLE PIE

PEACH PIE

PREP: 15 MIN. + STANDING BAKE: 40 MIN. + COOLING

Lemon juice adds a nice tang to this treat and also keeps the peaches from turning dark. Use frozen peaches to keep things simple, just be sure they are thawed and well drained.

ANNIE TOMPKINS ● DELTONA, FLORIDA

Pastry for double-crust pie (9 inches)
- 5 cups sliced peeled fresh peaches
- 1 tablespoon lemon juice
- 1/2 teaspoon almond extract
- 1 cup sugar
- 1/4 cup quick-cooking tapioca
- 1/4 teaspoon salt
- 2 tablespoons butter

- Line a 9-in. pie plate with the bottom crust. Trim pastry to 1 in. beyond edge of pie plate; set aside.

- In a large bowl, combine the peaches, lemon juice and extract. Add sugar, tapioca and salt; toss gently. Let stand for 15 minutes.

- Pour into crust; dot with butter. Roll out the remaining pastry; make a lattice crust. Seal and flute edges.

- Cover edges loosely with foil. Bake at 425° for 20 minutes. Remove foil; bake 20-30 minutes longer or until crust is golden brown and filling is bubbly. Cool on a wire rack.

YIELD: 6-8 SERVINGS.

EGGNOG PUMPKIN PIE

PREP: 40 MIN. + CHILLING BAKE: 50 MIN. + COOLING

This family favorite is a combination of three great pies. With its golden-brown crust, creamy filling and great flavor, it's a fitting finale to any meal.

LYN DILWORTH ● RANCHO CORDOVA, CALIFORNIA

- 1-1/4 cups all-purpose flour
- 1/4 teaspoon salt

EGGNOG PUMPKIN PIE

PEACH PIE

- 3 tablespoons shortening
- 3 tablespoons cold butter, cubed
- 3 to 4 tablespoons cold water

FILLING:
- 2 eggs
- 1 can (15 ounces) solid-pack pumpkin
- 1 cup eggnog
- 1/2 cup sugar
- 1 teaspoon ground cinnamon
- 1/2 teaspoon salt
- 1/2 teaspoon ground ginger
- 1/2 teaspoon ground nutmeg
- 1/4 teaspoon ground cloves

TOPPING:
- 1/2 cup packed brown sugar
- 2 tablespoons butter, softened
- 1/2 cup chopped pecans

- In a food processor, combine flour and salt; cover and pulse to blend. Add shortening and butter; cover and pulse until mixture resembles coarse crumbs. While processing, gradually add water until dough forms a ball. Wrap in plastic wrap. Refrigerate for 1 to 1-1/2 hours or until easy to handle.

- Roll out pastry to fit a 9-in. pie plate. Transfer pastry to pie plate. Trim pastry to 1/2 in. beyond edge of plate; flute edges.

- In a large bowl, whisk the eggs, pumpkin, eggnog, sugar, cinnamon, salt, ginger, nutmeg and cloves until blended. Pour into crust.

- In a small bowl, beat brown sugar and butter until crumbly, about 2 minutes. Stir in pecans; sprinkle over filling.

- Bake at 350° for 50-60 minutes or until a knife inserted near the center comes out clean. Cool on a wire rack. Refrigerate leftovers.

YIELD: 8 SERVINGS.

EDITOR'S NOTE: This recipe was tested with commercially prepared eggnog.

LEMONADE MERINGUE PIE

PREP: 30 MIN. **BAKE:** 15 MIN. + CHILLING

Lemonade concentrate and lemon juice give this refreshing pie an excellent citrus flavor. Add some lemon zest on top of the meringue for a pretty presentation.

KAY SEILER • GRENNVILLE, OHIO

3	eggs, separated
1	package (4.6 ounces) cook-and-serve vanilla pudding mix
1-1/4	cups milk
1	cup (8 ounces) sour cream
1/3	cup thawed lemonade concentrate
1	teaspoon lemon juice
1/4	teaspoon cream of tartar
6	tablespoons sugar
1	pastry shell (9 inches), baked

- Place egg whites in a small bowl; let stand at room temperature for 30 minutes. Meanwhile, in a large saucepan, combine the pudding mix, milk and sour cream until smooth. Cook and stir over medium heat until thickened and bubbly, about 5 minutes. Reduce heat; cook and stir 2 minutes longer.

- Remove from the heat. Gradually whisk 1 cup hot filling into egg yolks; return all to the pan. Bring to a gentle boil; cook and stir for 2 minutes. Remove from the heat. Gently stir in lemonade concentrate; keep warm.

- Add lemon juice and cream of tartar to egg whites; beat on medium speed until soft peaks form. Gradually beat in sugar, 1 tablespoon at a time, on high until stiff glossy peaks form and sugar is dissolved.

LEMON CHESS PIE

- Pour warm filling into pastry shell. Spread meringue over filling, sealing edges to pastry.

- Bake at 350° for 15-20 minutes or until the meringue is golden brown. Cool on a wire rack for 1 hour. Refrigerate for at least 3 hours before serving.

YIELD: 6-8 SERVINGS.

LEMON CHESS PIE

PREP: 15 MIN. **BAKE:** 35 MIN. + CHILLING

This creamy lemon pie cuts beautifully and has a smooth texture that melts in your mouth.

HANNAH LARUE RIDER • EAST POINT, KENTUCKY

1	sheet refrigerated pie pastry
4	eggs
1-1/2	cups sugar
1/2	cup lemon juice
1/4	cup butter, melted
1	tablespoon cornmeal
2	teaspoons all-purpose flour
1/8	teaspoon salt

- Unroll pastry on a lightly floured surface. Transfer to a 9-in. pie plate. Trim pastry to 1/2 in. beyond edge of plate; flute edges.

- In a large bowl, beat eggs for 3 minutes. Gradually add sugar; beat for 2 minutes or until mixture becomes thick and lemon-colored. Beat in the lemon juice, butter, cornmeal, flour and salt.

- Pour into pastry shell. Bake at 350° for 35-40 minutes or until a knife inserted near the center comes out clean. Cool on a wire rack for 1 hour. Refrigerate for at least 3 hours before serving.

YIELD: 6 SERVINGS.

LEMONADE MERINGUE PIE

RHUBARB BERRY PIE

PREP: 10 MIN. + STANDING BAKE: 45 MIN. + COOLING

*The delicious pairing of rhubarb and berries in this pie
is enhanced with a touch of almond and nutmeg.*

MRS. BILL LAWSON • TACOMA, WASHINGTON

- 3 cups diced fresh or frozen rhubarb, thawed and drained
- 1 cup fresh raspberries or strawberries
- 1/2 teaspoon lemon juice
- 1/8 teaspoon almond extract
- 1-1/3 cups sugar
- 3 tablespoons quick-cooking tapioca
- 1 tablespoon all-purpose flour
- 1/8 teaspoon salt
- 1/8 teaspoon ground nutmeg
- Pastry for double-crust pie (9 inches)
- 1 tablespoon butter

- In a large bowl, combine the rhubarb, berries, lemon juice and extract. Add the sugar, tapioca, flour, salt and nutmeg. Add to the fruit mixture; toss gently to coat. Let stand for 15 minutes.

- Line a 9-in. pie plate with bottom crust. Add filling. Dot with butter. Roll out remaining pastry to fit top of pie. Place over filling. Trim, seal and flute edges. Cut slits in pastry. Bake at 425° for 15 minutes. Reduce heat to 350°; bake 30-35 minutes longer or until crust is golden brown and filling is bubbly. Cool on a wire rack.

YIELD: 8 SERVINGS.

MAJESTIC CHERRY PIE

PREP: 20 MIN. + STANDING BAKE: 45 MIN. + COOLING

*Cherries are my favorite fruit so I had a lot of fun creating this
recipe. The sweet-tart pie was a big hit with my family, too.*

LOUISE PIPER • GARNER, IOWA

- 1 cup plus 1 tablespoon sugar, divided
- 2 tablespoons all-purpose flour
- 2 tablespoons quick-cooking tapioca
- 1/8 teaspoon salt
- 3-1/2 cups pitted fresh Rainier cherries
- 1 cup halved pitted fresh Bing cherries
- 1 tablespoon lemon juice
- 4-1/2 teaspoons butter
- Pastry for double-crust pie (9 inches)
- 2 teaspoons milk

- In a large bowl, combine 1 cup sugar, flour, tapioca and salt. Add cherries and lemon juice; toss to coat. Let stand for 15 minutes.

- Line a 9-in. pie plate with bottom pastry; trim even with edge of plate. Add the filling; dot with butter. Roll out remaining pastry to fit top of pie; place over filling. Trim, seal and flute edges. Cut slits in pastry. Brush with milk and sprinkle with remaining sugar.

- Cover edges loosely with foil. Bake at 400° for 45-50 minutes or until the crust is golden brown and filling is bubbly. Cool on a wire rack.

YIELD: 6-8 SERVINGS.

CRANBERRY-PECAN PEAR PIE

CRANBERRY-PECAN PEAR PIE
PREP: 30 MIN. BAKE: 55 MIN. + COOLING

*This is one of my favorite pies to make in the fall.
The spiced filling pairs perfectly with the buttery,
flaky crust. I always make two—one is never enough.*

FRANCES BENTHIN • SCIO, OREGON

2	cups all-purpose flour
1/2	teaspoon salt
3/4	cup cold butter
6	tablespoons cold water

FILLING:
4	cups sliced peeled fresh pears (about 5 medium)
1/2	cup chopped dried cranberries
1/2	cup chopped pecans
1/2	cup honey
1/4	cup butter, melted
3	tablespoons cornstarch
2	tablespoons grated lemon peel
1	teaspoon ground cinnamon
1	tablespoon milk
1-1/2	teaspoons sugar

- In a bowl, combine flour and salt. Cut in butter until crumbly. Gradually add water, tossing with a fork until dough forms a ball. Roll out half of the pastry to fit a 9-in. pie plate; transfer pastry to pie plate.

- In a bowl, combine the pears, cranberries, pecans, honey, butter, cornstarch, lemon peel and cinnamon; pour into crust. Roll out remaining pastry; make a lattice crust. Trim, seal and flute edges. Brush with milk; sprinkle with sugar.

- Bake at 400° for 15 minutes. Reduce heat to 350°; bake 40-50 minutes longer or until crust is golden brown and filling is bubbly. Cool on a wire rack.

YIELD: 8 SERVINGS.

BUMBLEBERRY PIE
PREP: 30 MIN. + CHILLING BAKE: 50 MIN.

*This pie has long been a hit at our lodge in the Canadian Rockies.
It is so popular it would be impossible to take it off the menu.*

BUFFALO MOUNTAIN LODGE • BANFF, ALBERTA

5-1/2	cups all-purpose flour
1/4	teaspoon salt
2	cups shortening
1	egg
1	tablespoon white vinegar
3/4	cup cold water

FILLING:
2	cups each fresh or frozen blueberries, raspberries and sliced strawberries
2	cups fresh or frozen chopped rhubarb
4	cups chopped peeled baking apples
2	cups sugar
2/3	cup all-purpose flour
2	tablespoons lemon juice

EGG WASH:
1	egg yolk
1	to 2 tablespoons water

- In a large bowl, combine flour and salt; cut in shortening until crumbly. Whisk the egg, vinegar and water; sprinkle over dry ingredients and toss. If needed, add more water, 1 tablespoon at a time, until the dough can be formed into a ball. Divide into four balls. Cover and chill for 30 minutes.

- On a lightly floured surface, roll out two balls to fit two 9-in. pie pans. Combine filling ingredients (partially thaw fruit if necessary); spoon into crust. Roll remaining pastry to fit pies; place over filling. Seal and flute edges.

- Beat yolk and water; brush over pies. Cut slits in top crust. Bake at 350° for 50-60 minutes or until golden brown.

YIELD: 16 SERVINGS (2 PIES).

ALL-AMERICAN STRAWBERRY PIE

PREP: 20 MIN. + CHILLING

*Sweet strawberries combine with tart blueberries to make
this lip-smacking red-white-and-blue treat. It was a
tradition for my grandmother to serve it every Fourth of July.*

ADA MARTIN • WELLESLEY, MASSACHUSETTS

3/4	cup sugar
1/2	cup all-purpose flour
1/4	teaspoon salt
3	cups milk
3	egg yolks, lightly beaten
2	tablespoons butter
1-1/2	teaspoons vanilla extract
1/2	pint heavy whipping cream

1-1/2 tablespoons confectioners' sugar
1 pie shell (9 inches), baked
1 pint fresh strawberries, halved
1 cup fresh or frozen blueberries

- In a 3-qt. saucepan, combine sugar, flour and salt. Add milk, stirring until smooth. Cook and stir over medium heat until thickened. Stir in small amount of milk mixture into yolks, then return all to saucepan. Cook, stirring for 2 minutes. Remove from the heat; stir in butter and vanilla. Cool 20 minutes.

- Pour into pie shell; chill several hours until firm. Whip cream and sugar; spread half over pie filling. Arrange berries on cream. Dollop or pipe remaining cream around edge of pie.

YIELD: 8 SERVINGS.

UPSIDE-DOWN APPLE CHEESE PIE

BERRY SPECIAL PIE
PREP/TOTAL TIME: 10 MIN.

I developed this refreshing dessert after tasting something similar at a restaurant. It's light and not too sweet and, thanks to a prepared crumb crust, it goes together quickly. We love it with raspberries, but you can substitute any fresh berry of your choice.

EVE GAUGER VARGAS • PRAIRIE VILLAGE, KANSAS

1/2 cup semisweet chocolate chips
1-1/2 teaspoons shortening
1 chocolate crumb crust (8 inches)
2 cups fresh raspberries
1 carton (8 ounces) frozen whipped topping, thawed

- In a microwave, melt the chocolate chips and shortening; stir until smooth. Spread over the bottom of pie crust. Top with raspberries and whipped topping. Refrigerate until serving.

YIELD: 6-8 SERVINGS.

BERRY SPECIAL PIE

UPSIDE-DOWN APPLE CHEESE PIE
PREP: 25 MIN. BAKE: 45 MIN.

Turn to this unique treat when you want to serve something different for dessert. The cheesecake–like pie features slices of tart apples and a delectable caramelized topping.

LISA DILWORTH • GRAND RAPIDS, MICHIGAN

2/3 cup chopped pecans
1/2 cup packed brown sugar
3 tablespoons butter, melted
Pastry for double-crust pie (9 inches)
1 package (8 ounces) cream cheese, softened
1/2 cup shredded cheddar cheese
1 tablespoon plus 1 cup sugar, divided
1 teaspoon vanilla extract
4 cups thinly sliced peeled tart apples
1/4 cup all-purpose flour
2 tablespoons lemon juice
2 teaspoons ground cinnamon
1/2 teaspoon ground ginger

- In a small bowl, combine the pecans, brown sugar and butter; spread into a greased 9-in. pie plate. Roll out one pastry to fit the pie plate; place over pecan mixture. Trim pastry even with edge of plate.

- In a small bowl, beat the cream cheese, cheddar cheese, 1 tablespoon sugar and vanilla until blended; spread over pastry. In large bowl, combine the apples, flour, lemon juice, cinnamon, ginger and remaining sugar; pour over cheese mixture.

- Roll out remaining pastry to fit top of pie; place over filling. Trim, seal and flute edges. Cut slits in top.

- Bake at 375° for 45-50 minutes or until golden brown. Cool for 5 minutes before inverting onto a serving plate. Serve warm.

YIELD: 6-8 SERVINGS.

MAKEOVER GRANDMA'S STRAWBERRY PIE

PREP: 40 MIN. + CHILLING

Shannon Chabes of Portage, Indiana wanted a lighter version of her grandma's classic summer pie. Our home economists came up with this one that offers all the flavor of the original but a fourth less fat and 152 fewer calories per slice. How sweet is that?

TASTE OF HOME TEST KITCHEN

1-1/4   cups all-purpose flour
2   tablespoons sugar
1/4   teaspoon salt
3   tablespoons cold butter
3   tablespoons canola oil
4   to 5 tablespoons buttermilk
FILLING:
1/2   cup sugar
2   tablespoons cornstarch
1   cup cold water
1   package (.3 ounce) sugar-free strawberry gelatin
4   cups sliced fresh strawberries
1/2   cup reduced-fat whipped topping

- In a large bowl, combine the flour, sugar and salt; cut in butter until crumbly. Gradually add oil, then buttermilk, tossing with a fork until dough forms a ball.

- Between two sheets of lightly floured waxed paper, roll out pastry to fit a 9-in. pie plate. Transfer pastry to pie plate; trim to 1/2 in. beyond edge of plate. Flute edges.

- Line unpricked pastry shell with a double thickness of heavy-duty foil. Bake at 450° for 8 minutes. Remove foil; bake 5-7 minutes longer or until lightly browned (cover edges with foil during the last few minutes to prevent overbrowning if necessary). Cool on a wire rack.

- For filling, in a small saucepan, combine the sugar and cornstarch. Stir in water until smooth. Bring to a boil,

MAKEOVER GRANDMA'S STRAWBERRY PIE

PEAR CRUMBLE PIE

stirring constantly. Cook and stir for 2 minutes or until thickened. Remove from the heat; stir in gelatin until dissolved. Let stand for 15 minutes.

- Place strawberries in a large bowl. Add gelatin mixture; gently toss to coat. Pour into crust. Refrigerate for 4 hours or until set. Garnish with whipped topping.

YIELD: 8 SERVINGS.

PEAR CRUMBLE PIE

PREP: 20 MIN. BAKE: 45 MIN. + COOLING

I couldn't really imagine a pear pie until I bit into this succulent dessert. The sweet crumb topping is wonderful, and the filling is a nice change from traditional apple. Try it with a scoop of frozen yogurt.

RUTH ANN STELFOX • RAYMOND, ALBERTA

1/3   cup sugar
3   tablespoons all-purpose flour
6   cups sliced peeled fresh pears
1   unbaked pastry shell (9 inches)
CRUMBLE TOPPING:
1/3   cup all-purpose flour
3   tablespoons brown sugar
1/4   teaspoon ground cinnamon
2   tablespoons cold butter

- In a large bowl, combine sugar and flour; add the pears and toss gently to coat. Spoon into pastry shell. In a small bowl, combine the flour, brown sugar and cinnamon; cut in butter until crumbly. Sprinkle over pie.

- Bake at 400° for 45-50 minutes or until pears are tender and topping is golden brown. Cover edges loosely with foil during the last 30 minutes to prevent overbrowning. Cool on a wire rack.

YIELD: 8 SERVINGS.

FUDGE PECAN PIE
PREP: 20 MIN. BAKE: 45 MIN.

The recipe for this fudgy pie can be easily doubled or even quadrupled to serve a large crowd. If you have extra slices leftover you can freeze them for a fast, tasty dessert to pull out on a moment's notice.

MILDRED SHERRER • FORT WORTH, TEXAS

1-1/2 ounces unsweetened chocolate
3 tablespoons butter
2 eggs
2 tablespoons all-purpose flour
1 cup sugar
1-1/2 tablespoons light corn syrup
1/2 teaspoon vanilla extract
Dash salt
3/4 cup chopped pecans
1 unbaked pie crust (9 inches)
Vanilla ice cream

• In a small saucepan over low heat, or in the microwave, melt chocolate and butter. Cool.

• In a small bowl, beat eggs until light; add flour and mix well. Add the sugar, corn syrup, vanilla and salt. Stir in melted chocolate and pecans. Pour into pie crust. Bake at 350° for 45 minutes or until top is crusty and filling is set.

• Serve warm with a scoop of ice cream.

YIELD: 8 SERVINGS.

OUT-OF-THIS-WORLD PIE (NO BAKE)
PREP/TOTAL TIME: 15 MIN.

Whipped topping conceals a glorious blend of cherries, pineapple, bananas and pecans in this pie. This was one of my father's favorites. I also like to serve it to special company.

LOUISE ROTH • STERLING, KANSAS

1 can (21 ounces) cherry pie filling
1 can (20 ounces) crushed pineapple, undrained
3/4 cup sugar
1 tablespoon cornstarch
1 package (3 ounces) raspberry gelatin
1/2 teaspoon red food coloring, optional
6 medium firm bananas, sliced
1 cup chopped pecans, toasted
2 pastry shells (9 inches), baked
1 carton (12 ounces) frozen whipped topping, thawed

• In a large saucepan, combine pie filling and pineapple. Combine sugar and cornstarch; add to fruit mixture. Cook and stir over medium heat until mixture comes to a boil. Cook and stir 1-2 minutes longer or until thickened.

• Remove from the heat. Add gelatin and food coloring if desired; mix well. Cool. Fold in bananas and pecans. Pour into the pie shells. Spread with whipped topping. Chill until serving.

YIELD: 2 PIES (6-8 SERVINGS EACH).

PEAR PRALINE PIE
PREP: 30 MIN. BAKE: 35 MIN. + COOLING

This treat is good served warm or at room temperature. We like it with scoops of vanilla ice cream or thick whipped cream on top. It's great with any meal or as an afternoon snack with a cup of hot joe or a cold glass of milk.

DIANE HALFERTY • CORPUS CHRISTI, TEXAS

1/4 cup all-purpose flour
1/2 teaspoon grated lemon peel
1/2 teaspoon ground ginger
4 medium pears, peeled and sliced
Pastry for double-crust pie (9 inches)
1 cup packed brown sugar
1/2 cup chopped pecans, toasted
1/4 cup butter, melted

• In a large bowl, combine the flour, lemon peel and ginger. Add pears; toss gently to coat.

• Line a 9-in. pie plate with bottom pastry; trim even with edge of plate. Add pear mixture. Combine the brown sugar, pecans and butter; sprinkle over pears.

• Roll out the remaining pastry to fit top of the pie; cut a decorative design in the center if desired. Place over filling; trim, seal and flute edges. (If using whole pastry on top without a decorative design, cut slits in pastry.)

• Bake at 400° for 35-45 minutes or until filling is bubbly and pears are tender (cover edges with foil during the last 15 minutes to prevent overbrowning if necessary). Cool completely on a wire rack. Store in the refrigerator.

YIELD: 6-8 SERVINGS.

PEAR-PRALINE PIE

CRAN-RASPBERRY PIE

PEACH STREUSEL PIE
PREP: 20 MIN. BAKE: 35 MIN.

You will want to save room for dessert when this peach sensation from our home economists is on the menu. Serve each warm, juicy slice with a scoop of vanilla ice cream for a fantastic ending to any meal.

TASTE OF HOME TEST KITCHEN

Pastry for single-crust pie (9 inches)
- 1/4 cup sugar
- 2 tablespoons cornstarch
- 2 tablespoons lemon juice
- 5 cups sliced fresh or frozen peaches, thawed

TOPPING:
- 2/3 cup packed brown sugar
- 1/2 cup granola cereal (without raisins)
- 1/4 cup all-purpose flour
- 1 teaspoon ground cinnamon
- 1/4 cup cold butter, cubed

Vanilla ice cream

- Line a 9-in. pie plate with pastry; flute edges. Line the pastry shell with a double thickness of heavy-duty foil. Bake at 450° for 5 minutes. Remove foil; bake 5 minutes longer. Cool on a wire rack.

- In a small bowl, combine the sugar, cornstarch, lemon juice and peaches. Spoon into pastry shell. In another bowl, combine brown sugar, granola, flour and cinnamon; cut in butter until crumbly. Sprinkle over filling.

- Bake at 375° for 35-40 minutes or until filling is bubbly. Cool on a wire rack. Serve warm with ice cream.

YIELD: 6-8 SERVINGS.

CRAN-RASPBERRY PIE
PREP: 20 MIN. + CHILLING

Sweet raspberry gelatin tames the tartness of cranberries and pineapple in this slice of heaven. The fluffy marshmallow–flavored topping makes it extra indulgent.

EDDIE STOTT • MT. JULIET, TENNESSEE

- 1 package (3 ounces) raspberry gelatin
- 1 cup boiling water
- 1 cup whole-berry cranberry sauce
- 1 can (8 ounces) unsweetened crushed pineapple, drained
- 1 graham cracker crust (9 inches)
- 2 cups miniature marshmallows
- 1/4 cup sweetened condensed milk
- 1/2 teaspoon vanilla extract
- 1 cup heavy whipping cream, whipped

- In a large bowl, dissolve gelatin in boiling water. Stir in cranberry sauce and pineapple. Chill until partially set. Pour into crust. Refrigerate until set.

- Meanwhile, in a heavy saucepan, combine marshmallows and milk. Cook and stir over medium-low heat until marshmallows are melted. Remove from the heat. Stir in vanilla. Transfer to a large bowl. Cover and let stand until cooled to room temperature.

- Whisk in a third of the whipped cream until smooth (mixture will be stringy at first). Fold in the remaining whipped cream. Spread over gelatin layer. Refrigerate until set.

YIELD: 6-8 SERVINGS.

HARVEST WATERMELON PIE
PREP: 30 MIN. BAKE: 40 MIN. + COOLING

You'll be surprised at the pleasant flavor watermelon rind adds to this unique pie. It's a refreshing and cool treat for a summer picnic or barbecue.

LORRI O'REILLY • ORLANDO, FLORIDA

- 3 cups chopped watermelon rind (peel and fruit removed)
- 1-1/3 cups (6 ounces) dried cranberries
- 3/4 cup chopped walnuts
- 1/3 cup cider vinegar
- 1/2 cup sugar
- 2 teaspoons pumpkin pie spice
- 1 teaspoon all-purpose flour
- 1/4 teaspoon salt

Pastry for double-crust pie (9 inches)
ORANGE GLAZE:
- 1/2 cup confectioners' sugar
- 2 teaspoons grated orange peel
- 1 tablespoon orange juice

CARAMEL-CRUNCH PUMPKIN PIE

shell. In a large bowl, whisk the eggs, pumpkin, extract, cinnamon, salt, mace, ginger and remaining brown sugar until blended; stir in cream.

- Pour into pastry shell. Cover edges loosely with foil. Bake at 400° for 10 minutes. Reduce heat to 350°; bake 40-45 minutes longer or until a knife inserted near the center comes out clean. Remove foil. Cool on a wire rack.

- Garnish with whipped cream and additional walnuts if desired. Refrigerate leftovers.

YIELD: 8 SERVINGS.

- Place watermelon rind in a saucepan and cover with water; bring to a boil. Reduce heat; simmer, uncovered, for 10 minutes or until rind is tender and translucent. Remove from the heat; drain. Place in a large bowl; add the cranberries, walnuts and vinegar.

- Combine sugar, pie spice, flour and salt; add to the rind mixture and stir well. Line a 9-in. pie plate with bottom pastry; trim the pastry even with edge. Add filling.

- Roll out remaining pastry; make a lattice crust. Seal and flute edges. Cover edges loosely with foil. Bake at 425° for 20 minutes. Remove foil; bake 20-25 minutes longer or until crust is golden brown.

- Combine glaze ingredients; spoon over hot pie. Cool on a wire rack.

YIELD: 6-8 SERVINGS.

CARAMEL-CRUNCH PUMPKIN PIE

PREP: 15 MIN. BAKE: 50 MIN. + COOLING

This extra-special holiday classic is both creamy and crunchy, thanks to the addition of whipping cream and chopped walnuts.

JUNE BLOMQUIST • EUGENE, OREGON

3/4	cup packed brown sugar, divided
1/2	cup finely chopped walnuts
2	tablespoons butter, melted
1	unbaked pastry shell (9 inches)
3	eggs
1	cup canned pumpkin
1	teaspoon rum extract
3/4	teaspoon ground cinnamon
1/2	teaspoon salt
1/2	teaspoon ground mace
1/4	teaspoon ground ginger
1-1/2	cups heavy whipping cream

Whipped cream and additional chopped walnuts, optional

- In a small bowl, combine 1/4 cup brown sugar, walnuts and butter until crumbly. Press onto bottom of pastry

STAR-STUDDED BLUEBERRY PIE

PREP: 30 MIN. BAKE: 45 MIN. + COOLING

Family and friends say this pleasing pie is better than a popular one served at a local restaurant. If desired, use gooseberries for half of the blueberries.

NANCY BARKER • SILVERTON, OREGON

4	cups fresh or frozen blueberries
1	cup sugar
1/4	cup quick-cooking tapioca
1	tablespoon lemon juice
1/4	teaspoon salt

Pastry for double-crust pie (9 inches)

2	tablespoons butter

- In a large bowl, combine the blueberries, sugar, tapioca, lemon juice and salt; toss gently. Let stand for 15 minutes. Line a 9-in. pie plate with bottom pastry; add filling. Dot with butter; flute edges.

- Cover edges loosely with foil. Bake at 400° for 25 minutes. Remove foil; bake 20-25 minutes longer or until set. Cool on a wire rack.

- From remaining pastry, cut out 15 large stars with a 2-in. cookie cutter and 15 small stars with a 1/2-in. cookie cutter. Place on an ungreased baking sheet. Bake at 350° for 5-10 minutes or until golden brown. Remove to wire racks to cool. Randomly place stars over cooled pie.

YIELD: 8 SERVINGS.

STAR-STUDDED BLUEBERRY PIE

STRAWBERRY APPLE PIE

STRAWBERRY APPLE PIE
PREP: 15 MIN. BAKE: 45 MIN.

I was baking an apple pie when I ran short on apples so I substituted strawberries. Everyone loved it!

DIANNE EBKE • PLYMOUTH, NEBRASKA

3-1/2   cups thinly sliced peeled Granny Smith apples (about 3 medium)
1-1/4   cups sliced fresh strawberries
1   tablespoon lemon juice
1/2   cup sugar
3   to 4 tablespoons all-purpose flour
Pastry for double-crust pie (9 inches)
TOPPING:
1/2   teaspoon sugar
1/8   teaspoon ground cinnamon
Whipped topping, optional

● In a large bowl, combine the apples and strawberries; drizzle with lemon juice. Combine sugar and flour; sprinkle over fruit and toss lightly.

● Line a 9-in. pie place with bottom pastry; trim even with edge of plate. Add filling. Roll out remaining pastry to fit top of pie; place over filling. Trim, seal and flute edges. Cut slits in top. Combine sugar and cinnamon; sprinkle over pastry. Cover edges loosely with foil.

● Bake at 450° for 10 minutes. Reduce heat to 350°; remove foil and bake 35-40 minutes longer or until crust is golden brown and filling is bubbly. Cool on a wire rack. Garnish with whipped topping if desired.

YIELD: 6-8 SERVINGS.

APRICOT MERINGUE PIE
PREP: 35 MIN. + CHILLING BAKE: 25 MIN. + COOLING

The meringue on this fabulous treat sits nice and high, while the sweet apricots retain a little of their chewy texture.

OLIVE RUMAGE • JACKSBORO, TEXAS

12   ounces dried apricots, chopped
1-1/2   cups water

2-1/2   cups sugar, divided
3   tablespoons cornstarch
1/4   teaspoon salt
4   eggs, separated
2   tablespoons butter
1/4   teaspoon cream of tartar
1   pastry shell (9 inches), baked

● In a saucepan, bring apricots and water to a boil. Reduce heat; simmer, uncovered, for 10 minutes or until apricots are softened.

● In a bowl, combine 2 cups sugar, cornstarch and salt; stir into apricot mixture. Bring to a boil. Reduce heat; cook and stir for 1 minute or until thickened. Remove from the heat; stir a small amount of hot filling into yolks. Return all to pan, stirring constantly. Bring to a gentle boil; cook and stir 1 minute longer or until glossy and clear. Remove from the heat; stir in butter. Keep warm.

● In a bowl, beat egg whites and cream of tartar on medium speed until soft peaks form. Gradually beat in remaining sugar, 1 tablespoon at a time, on high until stiff glossy peaks form and sugar is dissolved. Pour hot filling into crust. Spread meringue evenly over filling, sealing edges to crust.

● Bake at 325° for 25-30 minutes or until golden brown. Cool on a wire rack for 1 hour. Chill for at least 3 hours before serving. Refrigerate leftovers.

YIELD: 6-8 SERVINGS.

TRIPLE-FRUIT PIE
PREP: 25 MIN. BAKE: 50 MIN. + COOLING

This refreshing pie features juicy slices of peaches, apricots and nectarines baked inside a homemade golden-brown crust. It's irresistible on a warm summer day.

JANET LOOMIS • TERRY, MONTANA

2   cups all-purpose flour
1   teaspoon salt

TRIPLE-FRUIT PIE

RED RASPBERRY PIE

3/4 cup shortening
5 tablespoons cold water
1-2/3 cups each sliced peeled peaches, nectarines and apricots
1 tablespoon lemon juice
1/2 cup packed brown sugar
1/4 teaspoon ground ginger
1/4 teaspoon ground cinnamon
1 tablespoon butter

- In a small bowl, combine the flour and salt; cut in the shortening until crumbly. Gradually add water, tossing with a fork until dough forms a ball. Divide in half. On a lightly floured surface, roll out one portion to fit a 9-in. pie plate. Transfer pastry to plate; trim to 1/2 in. beyond edge.

- In a large bowl, combine the peaches, nectarines, apricots and lemon juice. Combine the brown sugar, ginger and cinnamon; sprinkle over fruit and toss gently to coat. Pour into crust; dot with butter.

- Roll out the remaining pastry to fit the top of pie; make decorative cutouts. Set cutouts aside. Place top crust over filling. Trim, seal and flute edges. Moisten cutouts with a small amount of water; place on top of pie.

- Cover edges loosely with foil. Bake at 375° for 25 minutes. Uncover; bake 25-30 minutes longer or until the crust is golden brown and the filling is bubbly. Cool pie on a wire rack.

YIELD: 6-8 SERVINGS.

RED RASPBERRY PIE

PREP: 20 MIN. + STANDING **BAKE**: 45 MIN. + COOLING

Fresh raspberries star in this luscious pie. A hint of lime nicely complements the sweet fruit.

PATRICIA MORROW • MAPLETON, MINNESOTA

1-1/2 cups plus 1/2 teaspoon sugar, divided
1/3 cup quick-cooking tapioca
1/4 teaspoon salt
6 cups fresh raspberries
1 teaspoon lime juice
Pastry for double-crust pie (9 inches)
1 tablespoon butter
1 teaspoon 2% milk

- In a large bowl, combine 1-1/2 cups sugar, tapioca and salt. Add raspberries and lime juice; toss gently to coat. Let stand for 15 minutes.

- Line a 9-in. pie plate with bottom pastry; trim even with edge of plate. Add the filling; dot with butter. Roll out the remaining pastry to fit top of pie; place over filling. Trim, seal and flute edges. Cut slits in top. Brush with milk; sprinkle with remaining sugar.

- Bake at 450° for 10 minutes. Reduce heat to 350°; remove foil and bake 35-40 minutes longer or until crust is golden brown and filling is bubbly. Cover the edges with foil during last 15 minutes to prevent overbrowning if necessary. Cool on a wire rack. Store in the refrigerator.

YIELD: 6-8 SERVINGS.

ORANGE COCONUT MERINGUE PIE

PREP: 35 MIN. BAKE: 15 MIN. + CHILLING

This tropical sensation bursts with citrus flavor. I won first place in two pie competitions with this recipe. It's one of my absolute favorites.

DAISY DUNCAN • STILLWATER, OKLAHOMA

- 1 cup sugar
- 3 tablespoons cornstarch
- 3 tablespoons all-purpose flour
- 1/4 teaspoon salt
- 1-1/2 cups water
- 3/4 cup orange juice
- 3 egg yolks, lightly beaten
- 3/4 cup flaked coconut
- 2 tablespoons butter
- 1 tablespoon grated orange peel
- 2 tablespoons lemon juice
- 1 pastry shell (9 inches), baked

MERINGUE:
- 3 egg whites
- 1/2 teaspoon vanilla extract
- 1/4 teaspoon cream of tartar
- 6 tablespoons sugar

- In a large saucepan, combine the sugar, cornstarch, flour and salt. Gradually stir in the water and orange juice until smooth. Cook and stir over medium-high heat until thickened and bubbly. Reduce heat; cook and stir 2 minutes longer. Remove from the heat.

- Stir a small amount of hot filling into egg yolks; return all to the pan, stirring constantly. Bring to a gentle boil; cook and stir 2 minutes longer. Remove from the heat. Stir in the coconut, butter and orange peel. Gently stir in lemon juice. Pour into pastry shell.

- In a small bowl, beat egg whites, vanilla and cream of tartar on medium speed until soft peaks form. Gradually beat in the sugar, 1 tablespoon at a time, on high until stiff glossy peaks form and sugar is dissolved. Spread evenly over hot filling, sealing edges to crust.

- Bake at 350° for 12-15 minutes or until the meringue is golden brown. Cool on a wire rack for 1 hour. Refrigerate for at least 3 hours before serving. Refrigerate leftovers.

YIELD: 6-8 SERVINGS.

OZARK BLUE-CRANBERRY PIE

PREP: 25 MIN. BAKE: 40 MIN.

My daughter and I live in the Missouri Ozarks, and we enjoy picking blueberries at a nearby Amish farm and freezing them for year-round use. I use the recipe often.

MARY MARSO • CROCKER, MISSOURI

CRUST:
- 2 cups all-purpose flour
- 1 teaspoon salt
- 1/2 teaspoon ground nutmeg
- 2/3 cup plus 2 tablespoons shortening, chilled
- 4 to 5 tablespoons ice water

FILLING:
- 1 can (14 ounces) whole-berry cranberry sauce
- 1/3 cup packed brown sugar
- 1/4 cup sugar
- 2 tablespoons all-purpose flour
- 2 tablespoons cornstarch
- 2 tablespoons orange juice
- 1/2 teaspoon grated orange peel
- 1/8 teaspoon salt
- 2 cups fresh or frozen blueberries
- 2 tablespoons butter

- For crust, combine flour, salt and nutmeg in a large bowl. Cut in shortening until mixture forms coarse crumbs. Add water, 1 tablespoon at a time, until ingredients are just moistened. Divide dough in half.

- Between sheets of waxed paper, roll each half into a circle large enough to fit a 9-in. pie pan. Press one circle into the pan; set aside the second circle.

frozen blueberries

It's fine to use frozen blueberries in place of fresh ones in pies and cobblers. Just be aware that frozen berries give off more juice, so when using those it's best to reduce the liquid and increase the thickener.

MAPLE PUMPKIN PIE

15 minutes to prevent overbrowning if necessary). Cool on a wire rack for 1 hour. Refrigerate overnight or until set.

- In a small bowl, beat the cream, confectioners' sugar, syrup and pumpkin pie spice until stiff peaks form. Pipe or dollop around the edge of pie. Sprinkle with pecans if desired. Refrigerate leftovers.

YIELD: 8 SERVINGS.

PEANUT BUTTER CRUMB APPLE PIE
PREP: 10 MIN. BAKE: 20 MIN. + COOLING

I use time-saving apple pie filling and a convenient pastry shell crust for this scrumptious pie. Dressed up with a crunchy streusel topping, it's a sweet afternoon pick-me-up or dinnertime finale.

BILLIE MOSS • WALNUT CREEK, CALIFORNIA

1	can (21 ounces) apple pie filling
1	teaspoon lemon juice
1	pastry shell (9 inches), baked
1/2	cup all-purpose flour
1/3	cup packed brown sugar
1	to 3 teaspoons grated lemon peel
1/2	teaspoon ground cinnamon
1/4	teaspoon ground nutmeg
6	tablespoons chunky peanut butter
2	tablespoons cold butter

- In a small bowl, combine the pie filling and lemon juice; spoon into pastry shell.
- In a large bowl, combine the flour, brown sugar, lemon peel, cinnamon and nutmeg; cut in peanut butter and butter until crumbly. Sprinkle over filling.
- Bake at 400° for 20-22 minutes or until the topping is lightly browned. Cool on a wire rack.

YIELD: 6-8 SERVINGS.

- For filling, combine the cranberry sauce, sugars, flour, cornstarch, orange juice, orange peel and salt in a large bowl. Mix well. Stir in blueberries. Spoon filling into pie crust; dot with butter. Place second crust over filling. Flute edges and cut slits to vent steam.
- Bake at 400° for 40 minutes or until the center is bubbly and the crust is golden brown. Cool to room temperature before serving.

YIELD: 6-8 SERVINGS.

MAPLE PUMPKIN PIE
PREP: 25 MIN. BAKE: 1 HOUR + CHILLING

Tired of traditional pumpkin pie? The maple syrup in this special delight is a subtle but terrific flavor enhancer.

LISA VARNER • GREENVILLE, SOUTH CAROLINA

2	eggs
1	can (15 ounces) solid-pack pumpkin
1	cup evaporated milk
3/4	cup sugar
1/2	cup maple syrup
1	teaspoon pumpkin pie spice
1/4	teaspoon salt

Pastry for single-crust pie (9 inches)
MAPLE WHIPPED CREAM:

1	cup heavy whipping cream
2	tablespoons confectioners' sugar
1	tablespoon maple syrup
1/4	teaspoon pumpkin pie spice

Chopped pecans, optional

- In a large bowl, combine the first seven ingredients; beat until smooth. Pour into crust.
- Bake at 425° for 15 minutes. Reduce heat to 350°. Bake 45-50 minutes longer or until crust is golden brown and top of pie is set (cover edges with foil during the last

PEANUT BUTTER CRUMB APPLE PIE

CREAM, CUSTARD & PUDDING PIES

THERE IS NOTHING MORE HEAVENLY THAN A RICH, VELVETY SLICE OF PIE. HERE YOU'LL FIND A HOST OF DREAMY SENSATIONS WHERE EACH BITE IS FILLED WITH SWEET, CREAMY SATISFACTION.

CHOCOLATE SILK PIE

BLUEBERRY CLOUD PIE (NO BAKE)

PREP: 15 MIN. + CHILLING

I always make two of these pies at a time because my husband and children devour them in a hurry! We can hardly wait until blueberries are in season to enjoy this fast, easy dessert.

DENISE HEATWOLE • WAYNESBORO, GEORGIA

1-1/4	cups miniature marshmallows
3	tablespoons butter, cubed
2-1/2	cups crisp rice cereal
1	package (3 ounces) berry blue gelatin
1/2	cup boiling water
1/2	cup cold water
2	cups heavy whipping cream
5	tablespoons confectioners' sugar
1-2/3	cups fresh blueberries

Additional fresh blueberries

- In a large saucepan, combine marshmallows and butter. Cook and stir over medium heat until marshmallows are melted. Stir in cereal. With greased hands, press onto the bottom and up the side of a greased 9-in. pie plate; set aside.

- In a large bowl, dissolve gelatin in boiling water; stir in cold water. Refrigerate until partially set, about 1 hour.

- In a small bowl, beat cream until it begins to thicken. Add sugar; beat until soft peaks form. Fold berries and 3 cups whipped cream into gelatin mixture. Pour into crust. Refrigerate pie and remaining whipped cream for up to 4 hours. Garnish with reserved cream and additional blueberries.

YIELD: 6-8 SERVINGS.

BLUEBERRY CLOUD PIE

CHERRY CHOCOLATE PIE

CHERRY CHOCOLATE PIE (NO BAKE)

PREP: 20 MIN. + CHILLING

I have a large family, and they like trying all of my cakes and pies. This sweet delight is one of their favorites, so I make it about six times a year.

BONNIE PHILLIPS • CEDAR HILL, MISSOURI

11	large marshmallows
1/3	cup milk
1	piece (3 ounces) milk chocolate candy bar, chopped
1	container (8 ounces) frozen whipped topping, thawed and divided
1	graham cracker crust (10 inches)
1	can (21 ounces) cherry pie filling

- In a large saucepan, combine the marshmallows, milk and chocolate. Cook and stir over medium-low heat until smooth. Cool completely.

- Fold 3/4 cup whipped topping into chocolate mixture. Pour into prepared crust. Cover and refrigerate for at least 30 minutes. Top with the cherry pie filling and remaining whipped topping. Cover and refrigerate for 8 hours or overnight.

YIELD: 8 SERVINGS.

EDITOR'S NOTE: This recipe uses half of a 6-ounce milk chocolate candy bar.

FLUFFY LEMON PIE

PREP: 15 MIN. + CHILLING

This pie takes minutes to prepare and is the perfect light dessert. I make it often since my husband loves it, and we both need to watch our fat and cholesterol intake. My son, who's diabetic, loves the tangy, lemon flavor.

CAROLYN BAUERS • NORFOLK, VIRGINIA

- 1   package (1 ounce) sugar-free instant vanilla pudding mix
- 1   teaspoon sugar-free lemonade soft drink mix
- 1   cup cold fat-free milk
- 1   carton (8 ounces) frozen reduced-fat whipped topping, thawed, divided
- 1   reduced-fat graham cracker crust (8 inches)

- Combine pudding mix and soft drink mix. In a small bowl, whisk milk and pudding mixture for 2 minutes. Let stand for 2 minutes (pudding will be stiff).
- Fold in half of the whipped topping. Spread into crust. Top with remaining whipped topping. Cover and chill for 2-3 hours or until set.

YIELD: 8 SERVINGS.

EDITOR'S NOTE: This recipe was prepared with Crystal Light Drink Mix.

FLUFFY LEMON PIE

CRANBERRY CHIFFON PIE

PREP/TOTAL TIME: 30 MIN.

I like to serve this refreshing cranberry dessert after a hearty meal. The rosy color is a pretty addition to the table, especially during the holidays.

IVA COMBS • MEDFORD, OREGON

- 1   cup all-purpose flour
- 2   tablespoons sugar
- 1/2 cup cold butter
- 1/2 cup finely chopped walnuts

FILLING:
- 1   package (3 ounces) cranberry or strawberry gelatin
- 1/2 cup boiling water
- 1   cup whole-berry cranberry sauce
- 3/4 cup cranberry juice
- 1   tablespoon grated orange peel
- 1   cup heavy whipping cream, whipped

- In a bowl, combine the flour and sugar. Cut in butter until crumbly. Stir in walnuts. Press onto the bottom and up the sides of a greased 10-in. pie plate. Bake at 375° for 14-16 minutes or until set and edges are lightly browned. Cool on a wire rack.
- For filling, in a bowl, dissolve gelatin in water. Stir in the cranberry sauce, cranberry juice and orange peel. Cover and refrigerate until slightly thickened, about 1 hour. Fold in whipped cream. Pour into crust. Refrigerate for at least 3 hours.

YIELD: 6-8 SERVINGS.

CANDY BAR PIE

PREP/TOTAL TIME: 20 MIN.

This is one of my favorite pies to make. It is so easy with very few ingredients. For a change of pace, try chocolate bars with toffee bits or peanuts.

ROSALIND HAMILTON • IOWA, LOUISIANA

- 6   chocolate bars with almonds (1.45 ounces each)
- 1   carton (8 ounces) frozen whipped topping, thawed
- 3   teaspoons vanilla extract
- 1   graham cracker crust (9 inches)

Shaved chocolate, optional

- In a microwave, melt chocolate bars; stir until blended. Quickly fold in whipped topping. Stir in vanilla.
- Spoon into pie crust. Garnish with shaved chocolate if desired. Chill until serving.

YIELD: 6-8 SERVINGS.

CREAMY BANANA-BERRY PIE

CREAMY BANANA-BERRY PIE

PREP: 30 MIN. + CHILLING

(NO BAKE)

*Cool, creamy and topped with bananas and fresh
blueberries, this attractive pie is lighter than
air and will melt in your mouth.*

TASTE OF HOME TEST KITCHEN

1	sheet refrigerated pie pastry
1/4	cup chopped pecans
1-1/4	cups cold fat-free milk
1/2	cup reduced-fat sour cream

Sugar substitute equivalent to 1/4 cup sugar

1	package (.9 ounce) sugar-free instant banana pudding mix
2	cups reduced-fat whipped topping
1	tablespoon lemon juice
2	medium bananas
1/3	cup fresh blueberries

● Unroll pastry on a lightly floured surface. Sprinkle with pecans; lightly roll pecans into pastry. Transfer to a 9-in. pie plate. Line unpricked pastry shell with a double thickness of heavy-duty foil. Bake at 450° for 8 minutes. Remove foil; bake 5 minutes longer. Cool on a wire rack.

● In a small bowl, combine the milk, sour cream and sugar substitute. Gradually whisk in dry pudding mix. Fold in whipped topping.

● Place lemon juice in a small bowl. Slice the bananas into juice and stir gently to coat. Set aside 1/3 cup; spoon remaining banana slices into the crust. Top with pudding mixture, blueberries and reserved banana slices. Cover and refrigerate for 30 minutes before serving.

YIELD: 8 SERVINGS.

EDITOR'S NOTE: This recipe was tested with Splenda no-calorie sweetener.

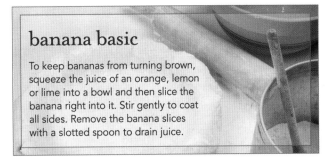

banana basic

To keep bananas from turning brown, squeeze the juice of an orange, lemon or lime into a bowl and then slice the banana right into it. Stir gently to coat all sides. Remove the banana slices with a slotted spoon to drain juice.

COCONUT PISTACHIO PIE

COCONUT PISTACHIO PIE

PREP: 20 MIN. + CHILLING

Our panel of tasters simply loved the crust of lightly toasted coconut that pairs so well with green pistachio pudding in this quick and easy pie.

TASTE OF HOME TEST KITCHEN

2-1/2   cups flaked coconut, lightly toasted
1/3   cup butter, melted
2   cups cold milk
2   packages (3.4 ounces each) instant pistachio pudding mix
1   cup whipped topping
2   tablespoons chopped pistachios, optional

- In a small bowl, combine the coconut and butter. Press onto the bottom and up the sides of a greased 9-in. pie plate. Refrigerate for at least 30 minutes or until firm.

- In a small bowl, whisk the milk and pudding mixes for 2 minutes. Spread 1-1/2 cups over crust. Fold whipped topping into remaining pudding; spread over the pie. Sprinkle with pistachios if desired. Cover and refrigerate for at least 2 hours.

YIELD: 8 SERVINGS.

BLUEBERRY FLUFF PIE

PREP: 25 MIN. + CHILLING

This light dessert is a perfect ending to a meal. The original recipe from my mother called for sliced peaches, which are also good.

SHIRLEY DIEROLF • STROUDSBURG, PENNSYLVANIA

20   large marshmallows
1/4   cup milk
4   cups fresh blueberries, divided
1   carton (8 ounces) frozen whipped topping, thawed
1   pastry shell (9 inches), baked

- In a heavy saucepan, combine marshmallows and milk. Cook and stir over medium-low heat until marshmallows are melted and mixture is smooth. Cool for 8-10 minutes, stirring several times.

- Stir in 3-1/2 cups blueberries. Set aside 1/2 cup whipped topping; fold the remaining topping into the blueberry mixture. Pour into the crust. Refrigerate for at least 2 hours. Garnish with the remaining blueberries and reserved topping.

YIELD: 8 SERVINGS.

CREAMY PINEAPPLE PIE

PREP/TOTAL TIME: 10 MIN.

This refreshing dessert is simple to make and impressive to serve. It's one of our favorite items to include on a summer menu.

SHARON BICKETT • CHESTER, SOUTH CAROLINA

- 1 can (14 ounces) sweetened condensed milk
- 1 can (8 ounces) crushed pineapple, undrained
- 1/4 cup lemon juice
- 1 carton (8 ounces) frozen whipped topping, thawed
- 1 prepared graham cracker crust (9 inches)

● In a bowl, mix milk, pineapple and lemon juice. Fold in the whipped topping. Pour into the crust. Chill until ready to serve.

YIELD: 8 SERVINGS.

CREAM CHEESE LIME PIE

PREP: 15 MIN. COOK: 20 MIN. + CHILLING

A shortbread cookie crust and a lime filling offer a delicious taste twist from typical lemon pie. You can substitute graham cracker crumbs for the cookie crumbs.

TASTE OF HOME TEST KITCHEN

- 1-1/2 cups shortbread cookies
- 3 tablespoons butter, melted

LIME FILLING:
- 1 cup sugar
- 1/4 cup cornstarch
- 3 tablespoons all-purpose flour
- 1/4 teaspoon salt
- 2 cups water
- 3 egg yolks, beaten
- 1 tablespoon butter
- 1 teaspoon grated lime peel

Green liquid food coloring, optional
- 1/4 cup lime juice

CREAM CHEESE FILLING:
- 1 package (8 ounces) cream cheese, softened
- 1/2 cup confectioners' sugar
- 2 teaspoons lime juice
- 1 cup whipped topping

● Combine cookie crumbs and butter; press onto the bottom and up the sides of an ungreased 9-in. pie plate. Bake at 375° for 8-10 minutes or until crust just begins to brown. Cool on a wire rack.

● For lime filling, combine the sugar, cornstarch, flour and salt in a saucepan. Stir in water until smooth. Cook and stir over medium-high heat until thickened and bubbly. Reduce heat; cook and stir 2 minutes longer. Remove

from the heat. Stir a small amount for hot filling into egg yolks; return all to the pan, stirring constantly. Bring to a gentle boil; cook and stir 2 minutes longer. Remove from the heat. Stir in butter, lime peel and food coloring if desired. Gently stir in lime juice. Cool to room temperature without stirring.

● For the cream cheese filling, beat the cream cheese, confectioners' sugar and lime juice in a small bowl until smooth. Fold in whipped topping. Spread evenly in crust; top with the lime filling. Refrigerate for 3 hours or until firm. Refrigerate leftovers.

YIELD: 6-8 SERVINGS.

APPLE CREAM CHEESE PIE

PREP: 20 MIN. + CHILLING

With just a handful of ingredients and convenient pie filling, this fluffy, cream cheese pie is a great dessert for time-pressed cooks. For a little tarter taste, substitute cherry pie filling for the apple.

LINDA DUNCAN • JUNCTION CITY, OREGON

- 1 package (8 ounces) cream cheese, softened
- 1/2 cup confectioners' sugar
- 1 teaspoon vanilla extract
- 1 carton (8 ounces) frozen whipped topping, thawed
- 1 graham cracker crust (9 inches)
- 1-3/4 cups apple pie filling

Dash ground cinnamon

● In a large bowl, beat cream cheese and confectioners' sugar until smooth. Beat in vanilla. Fold in whipped topping.

● Pour into crust. Top with the pie filling and sprinkle with cinnamon. Refrigerate for at least 2 hours before serving.

YIELD: 6-8 SERVINGS.

APPLE CREAM CHEESE PIE

EGGNOG PIE

EGGNOG PIE

PREP: 15 MIN. + CHILLING

A dear friend always received rave reviews when she served this easy pie. So I knew I needed the recipe!

PATTY ADLER • WRAY, COLORADO

2 cups eggnog
1 cup milk
1 package (4.6 ounces) cook-and-serve vanilla pudding mix
1 tablespoon rum or 1/2 teaspoon rum extract
1/8 teaspoon ground nutmeg
1 pastry shell (9 inches), baked
Whipped topping and additional ground nutmeg, optional

● In a large saucepan, cook the eggnog, milk and pudding mix over medium heat until thickened and bubbly. Remove from the heat and cool slightly. Stir in rum and nutmeg. Pour pudding mixture into crust. Chill until set. Garnish with whipped topping and sprinkle with nutmeg if desired.

YIELD: 8 SERVINGS.

EDITOR'S NOTE: This recipe was tested with commercially prepared eggnog.

REFRESHING LIME PIE

PREP: 15 MIN. + CHILLING

Everyone can enjoy a fluffy slice of this tart, refreshing pie. The recipe calls for reduced-fat and sugar-free ingredients so it's a real gem for diabetics.

MILDRED BAKER • YOUNGSTOWN, OHIO

1 envelope unflavored gelatin
1/2 cup cold water
1 package (.3 ounces) sugar-free lime gelatin

1/2 cup boiling water
3 cups (24 ounces) fat-free reduced-sugar key lime pie yogurt or lemon yogurt
1-1/2 cups reduced-fat whipped topping
1 shortbread crust (8 inches)

● In a small bowl, sprinkle gelatin over cold water; let stand for 1 minute. In another bowl, dissolve lime gelatin in boiling water; stir in unflavored gelatin until dissolved. Refrigerate for 10 minutes.

● Stir in yogurt. Chill until partially set. Fold in whipped topping. Pour into crust. Chill until firm.

YIELD: 8 SERVINGS.

RASPBERRY PATCH CREAM PIE

PREP: 35 MIN. + CHILLING

Our family loves raspberries, and this pie keeps the flavor and firmness of the berries intact. The combination of the berry-gelatin and cream cheese layers keeps everyone coming back for seconds.

ALLISON ANDERSON • RAYMOND, WASHINGTON

1 cup graham cracker crumbs
1/2 cup sugar
5 tablespoons butter, melted
FILLING:
1 package (8 ounces) cream cheese, softened
1/4 cup confectioners' sugar
2 teaspoons milk
1 teaspoon vanilla extract
TOPPING:
3/4 cup sugar
3 tablespoons cornstarch
1-1/3 cups cold water
1/4 cup raspberry gelatin powder
3 cups fresh raspberries

● In a small bowl, combine the cracker crumbs, sugar and butter. Press onto the bottom and up the sides of an ungreased 9-in. pie plate. Bake at 350° for 9-11 minutes or until set. Cool on a wire rack.

● For filling, in a small bowl, combine the cream cheese, confectioners' sugar, milk and vanilla. Carefully spread over crust.

● For topping, in a small saucepan, combine the sugar, cornstarch and water until smooth. Bring to a boil; cook and stir for 2 minutes or until thickened. Remove from the heat; stir in the gelatin until dissolved. Cool to room temperature. Refrigerate until slightly thickened.

● Arrange raspberries over filling. Spoon gelatin mixture over berries. Refrigerate until set.

YIELD: 6-8 SERVINGS.

RASPBERRY PATCH CREAM PIE

STRAWBERRY CUSTARD PIES

STRAWBERRY CUSTARD PIES

PREP: 35 MIN. + CHILLING

These pies were a spring special at a restaurant where I used to work. They're a great make-ahead dessert that will appeal to many. I whip up a few to bring to church suppers and potlucks.

CAROLINE PARK • PRITCHARD, BRITISH COLUMBIA

4-1/2	cups sugar
3/4	cup cornstarch
4-1/2	cups cold water
3	packages (3 ounces each) strawberry gelatin
1	tablespoon lemon juice
6	packages (3 ounces each) cook-and-serve vanilla pudding mix
6	pastry shells (9 inches), baked
3	pounds fresh strawberries, halved

Whipped cream, optional

● In a large saucepan, combine sugar and cornstarch; gradually stir in water until smooth. Bring to a boil; cook and stir for 2 minutes or until thickened. Remove from the heat. Stir in the gelatin and lemon juice until gelatin is dissolved. Cool to room temperature.

● Prepare pudding mixes according to package directions. Pour into pastry shells. Top with strawberries. Carefully spoon gelatin mixture over berries. Refrigerate until set. Garnish with whipped cream if desired.

YIELD: 6 PIES (8 SERVINGS EACH).

LEMON CREAM CHEESE PIE

PREP: 45 MIN. + CHILLING

This recipe is served at Al's Oasis in Chamberlain, South Dakota. It is so wonderful that I needed the recipe to be able to duplicate it successfully.

RENIE SMITH • RAPID CITY, SOUTH DAKOTA

1	cup sugar
1/2	cup cornstarch
1/8	teaspoon salt
2-1/2	cups cold water
3	eggs yolks, lightly beaten

3 tablespoons butter
2/3 cup lemon juice, divided
1 package (8 ounces) cream cheese, softened
1 can (14 ounces) sweetened condensed milk
1 package (3.4 ounces) lemon-flavored instant pudding mix
2 pie shells (9 inches), baked
Whipped cream
Lemon slices

- In a large saucepan, combine the sugar, cornstarch and salt. Stir in the water until smooth. Cook and stir over medium-high heat until thickened and bubbly. Reduce heat; cook and stir 2 minutes longer. Remove from the heat. Stir a small amount of hot filling into egg yolks; return all to pan, stirring constantly. Bring to a gentle boil; cook and stir 2 minutes longer.

- Remove from the heat. Stir in the butter. Gently stir in 1/3 cup lemon juice. Cool for several hours or overnight.

- In a large bowl, beat the cream cheese and condensed milk until smooth. Stir in pudding mix and remaining lemon juice.

- Fold into chilled lemon filling. Divide and spoon into baked pie shells. Refrigerate for several hours. Garnish with whipped cream and lemon slices.

YIELD: 12-16 SERVINGS.

CRANBERRY CUSTARD MERINGUE PIE

PREP: 35 MIN. BAKE: 15 MIN. + CHILLING

I love to serve this pie around the holidays while my family visits. My grandchildren call it the red-colored pie with the fluffy topping. Everyone loves the tangy cranberries and sweet, creamy custard.

LEE BREMSON • KANSAS CITY, MISSOURI

3 eggs, separated
Pastry for single-crust pie (9 inches)
1-3/4 cups fresh or frozen cranberries
1 tablespoon grated orange peel
1-1/4 cups plus 6 tablespoons sugar, divided
1 cup water
Dash salt
Dash ground cinnamon
4 teaspoons plus 1/4 cup cornstarch, divided
1/4 cup orange juice
2 cups 2% milk, divided
1 tablespoon butter
1 teaspoon vanilla extract
1/4 teaspoon cream of tartar

- Place egg whites in a small bowl; let stand at room temperature for 30 minutes.

- Meanwhile, line a 9-in. pie plate with pastry; trim and flute edges. Line pastry shell with a double thickness of heavy-duty foil. Bake at 450° for 8 minutes. Remove foil; bake 5 minutes longer. Cool on a wire rack.

- In a small saucepan, combine the cranberries, orange peel, 1/2 cup sugar, water, salt and cinnamon. Cook over medium heat until the berries pop, about 15 minutes. Combine 4 teaspoons cornstarch and orange juice until smooth; stir into the cranberry mixture. Bring to a boil; cook and stir for 1-2 minutes or until thickened. Remove from the heat; set aside.

- In another small saucepan, heat 3/4 cup sugar and 1-3/4 cups milk until bubbles form around sides of pan. In a small bowl, combine remaining cornstarch and milk. Whisk in egg yolks until blended. Add a small amount of hot milk mixture; return all to pan, whisking constantly.

- Whisk vigorously over medium heat as mixture begins to thicken (mixture will become very thick). Bring to a boil; whisk 2 minutes longer. Remove from the heat; whisk in butter and vanilla. Transfer custard to crust; spread evenly with reserved cranberry mixture.

- Add cream of tartar to egg whites; beat on medium speed until soft peaks form. Gradually beat in remaining sugar, 1 tablespoon at a time, on high until stiff glossy peaks form and sugar is dissolved. Spread evenly over filling, sealing edges to crust.

- Bake at 350° for 12-15 minutes or until the meringue is golden brown. Cool on a wire rack for 1 hour. Refrigerate overnight.

YIELD: 8 SERVINGS.

CRANBERRY CUSTARD MERINGUE PIE

COCONUT CHIFFON PIE
PREP: 30 MIN. + CHILLING

This silky pie is pure heaven.
A refreshing slice is good after a hearty meal.

KRISTINE FRY • FENNIMORE, WISCONSIN

1	unbaked pastry shell (9 inches)
1	envelope unflavored gelatin
1/4	cup cold water
1/2	cup sugar
1/4	cup all-purpose flour
1/2	teaspoon salt
1-1/2	cups milk
3/4	teaspoon vanilla extract
1/4	teaspoon almond extract
1	cup heavy whipping cream, whipped
1	cup flaked coconut

Shaved fresh coconut, optional

- Line unpricked pastry shell with a double thickness of heavy-duty foil. Bake at 450° for 8 minutes. Remove foil; bake 5 minutes longer. Cool on a wire rack.

- Sprinkle gelatin over cold water; let stand for 1 minute. In a small saucepan, combine the sugar, flour and salt. Gradually stir in milk until smooth. Cook and stir over medium-low heat until mixture comes to a boil; cook and stir 1 minute longer or until thickened.

- Remove from the heat. Whisk in the gelatin mixture until dissolved. Transfer to a large bowl. Refrigerate until slightly thickened, about 30 minutes.

- Add extracts; beat on medium speed for 1 minute. Fold in whipped cream and flaked coconut. Spread into pie crust. Refrigerate for at least 3 hours before serving. Garnish with shaved fresh coconut if desired.

YIELD: 6-8 SERVINGS.

MAPLE CREAM PIE
PREP: 45 MIN. + CHILLING

New York is one of the nation's top producers of maple syrup.
I often serve this pie featuring this sweet ingredient.
A sprinkling of almonds on top adds a decorative touch.

EMMA MAGIELDA • AMSTERDAM, NEW YORK

Pastry for single-crust pie (9 inches)

1/4	cup cornstarch
1/4	teaspoon salt
1-3/4	cups milk, divided
3/4	cup plus 1 tablespoon maple syrup, divided
2	egg yolks, lightly beaten
2	tablespoons butter
1	cup heavy whipping cream

Sliced almonds, toasted

- Line a 9-in. pie plate with pastry; trim to 1/2 in. beyond edge of plate. Flute edges. Line unpricked pastry shell with a double thickness of heavy-duty foil. Bake at 450° for 8 minutes. Remove foil; bake 5 minutes longer. Cool on a wire rack.

- For filling, combine cornstarch and salt in a large saucepan. Stir in 1/2 cup milk until smooth. Gradually stir in remaining milk and 3/4 cup maple syrup. Cook and stir over medium heat until thickened and bubbly. Reduce heat; cook and stir 2 minutes longer. Remove from the heat. Stir a small amount of hot filling into the egg yolks; return all to the pan, stirring constantly. Bring to a gentle boil; cook and stir 2 minutes longer. Remove from heat. Gently stir in butter. Cool to room temperature without stirring.

- In a chilled small bowl, beat cream on high speed until stiff peaks form. Fold 1 cup cream into cooled filling; spoon into crust. Fold remaining syrup into remaining cream; frost top of pie. Refrigerate overnight. Garnish with toasted almonds. Refrigerate leftovers.

YIELD: 8 SERVINGS.

MAPLE CREAM PIE

GRASSHOPPER PIE

GRASSHOPPER PIE
PREP: 15 MIN. + CHILLING

This pie has been a long-standing Christmas tradition in our family. We love it so much though that I now make it throughout the year!

MELISSA SOKASITS • WARRENVILLE, ILLINOIS

- 1-1/2 cups cold milk
- 1 package (3.9 ounces) instant chocolate pudding mix
- 2-3/4 cups whipped topping, divided
- 1 package (4.67 ounces) mint Andes candies, chopped, divided
- 1 chocolate crumb crust (9 inches)
- 1/4 teaspoon mint extract
- 2 drops green food coloring, optional

- In a small bowl, whisk the milk and pudding mix for 2 minutes. Let stand for 2 minutes or until soft-set. Fold in 3/4 cup whipped topping. Fold in 3/4 cup candies. Spoon into crust.

- In another bowl, combine extract and remaining whipped topping; add food coloring if desired. Spread over pudding layer; sprinkle with remaining candies. Cover and refrigerate for 4 hours or until set.

YIELD: 8 SERVINGS.

easy chocolate curls

It's a cinch to add a pretty chocolate garnish to pies. Use a vegetable peeler to "peel" curls from a solid block of chocolate. If you get only shavings, slightly warm your chocolate as it may be too hard.

CHOCOLATE SILK PIE
PREP: 30 MIN. + CHILLING

This quick, creamy chocolate pie not only melts in your mouth, it also melts any and all resistance to dessert!

MARY RELYEA • CANASTOTA, NEW YORK

- 1 unbaked pastry shell (9 inches)
- 1 jar (7 ounces) marshmallow creme
- 1 cup (6 ounces) semisweet chocolate chips
- 1/4 cup butter, cubed
- 2 ounces unsweetened chocolate
- 2 tablespoons strong brewed coffee
- 1 cup heavy whipping cream, whipped

TOPPING:
- 1 cup heavy whipping cream
- 2 tablespoons confectioners' sugar

Chocolate curls, optional

- Line unpricked pastry shell with a double thickness of heavy-duty foil. Bake at 450° for 8 minutes. Remove foil; bake 5 minutes longer. Cool on a wire rack.

- Meanwhile, in a heavy saucepan, combine marshmallow creme, chocolate chips, butter, unsweetened chocolate and coffee; cook and stir over low heat until chocolate is melted and mixture is smooth. Cool. Fold in whipped cream; pour into crust.

- For topping, in a large bowl, beat cream until it begins to thicken. Add confectioners' sugar; beat until stiff peaks form. Spread over chocolate filling. Refrigerate for at least 3 hours before serving. Garnish with chocolate curls if desired.

YIELD: 6-8 SERVINGS.

CHOCOLATE SILK PIE

CRANBERRY CREAM CHEESE PIE

CRANBERRY CREAM CHEESE PIE

PREP: 40 MIN. + CHILLING

*Fluffy and colorful, this pie is a
Christmas tradition at our house. Even after a
big meal, we all find room for this layered treat.*

CATHY WOOD • SALIDA, COLORADO

    1   cup fresh or frozen cranberries, divided
    1   package (.3 ounce) sugar-free raspberry gelatin
Sugar substitute equivalent to 1/3 cup plus 1 tablespoon sugar, divided
1-1/4   cups cranberry juice
    1   package (8 ounces) reduced-fat cream cheese
    1   tablespoon fat-free milk
    1   teaspoon vanilla extract
    1   pastry shell (9 inches), baked
    8   tablespoons fat-free whipped topping

- Place half of the cranberries in a food processor. Cover and process until ground; set aside. In a small bowl, combine the gelatin and 1/3 cup sugar substitute. In a small saucepan, bring cranberry juice to a boil. Pour over gelatin mixture; stir until dissolved. Stir in the ground cranberries and remaining whole cranberries. Cover and refrigerate until slightly thickened, about 40 minutes.

- In a small bowl, combine cream cheese and remaining sugar substitute. Beat in milk and vanilla. Spread into pastry shell.

- Transfer gelatin mixture to a bowl; beat for 4-5 minutes or until foamy. Spoon over cream cheese layer. Cover and refrigerate for at least 2 hours or until firm. Garnish each piece with 1 tablespoon whipped topping.

YIELD: 8 SERVINGS.

EDITOR'S NOTE: This recipe was tested with Splenda no-calorie sweetener.

SOUR CREAM RAISIN PIE

PREP: 15 MIN. BAKE: 50 MIN. + COOLING

*This recipe has been in our family since the 1860s.
For us, this pie is as essential for Thanksgiving dinner
as turkey, dressing and mashed potatoes!*

TRISH REMPE • SUPERIOR, NEBRASKA

Pastry for double-crust pie (9 inches)
    2   eggs
    1   cup (8 ounces) sour cream
  3/4   cup sugar
    2   tablespoons cider vinegar
    1   teaspoon ground cinnamon
  1/2   teaspoon ground cloves
  1/8   teaspoon salt
    1   cup raisins

- Line a 9-in. pie plate with bottom of pastry; trim even with the edge of plate. In a small bowl, beat the eggs on medium speed for 1 minute. Add the sour cream, sugar, vinegar, cinnamon, cloves and salt and mix well. Stir in raisins. Pour into pastry shell.

- Roll out remaining pastry to fit top of pie. Place over filling; trim, seal and flute edges. Cut slits in pastry.

- Bake at 400° for 10 minutes. Reduce heat to 350° and remove foil. Bake 40-45 minutes longer or until golden brown. Cover edges with foil during the last 15 minutes to prevent overbrowning if necessary. Cool on a wire rack. Refrigerate leftovers.

YIELD: 6-8 SERVINGS.

NO-COOK COCONUT PIE

PREP/TOTAL TIME: 15 MIN.

A quick meal doesn't have to go without dessert! This creamy no-bake pie is simply irresistible.

JEANETTE FUEHRING • CONCORDIA, MISSOURI

2	packages (3.4 ounces each) instant vanilla pudding mix
2-3/4	cups cold milk
1	teaspoon coconut extract
1	carton (8 ounces) frozen whipped topping, thawed
1/2	cup flaked coconut
1	graham cracker crust (9 inches)

Toasted coconut

- In a large bowl, beat the dry pudding mixes, milk and coconut extract on low speed until combined. Beat on high for 2 minutes. Fold in the whipped topping and coconut. Pour into the crust. Sprinkle with the toasted coconut. Chill until ready to serve. Refrigerate leftovers.

YIELD: 6-8 SERVINGS.

NO-COOK COCONUT PIE

GINGERSNAP PUMPKIN PIE

GINGERSNAP PUMPKIN PIE

PREP: 30 MIN. + CHILLING

The fantastic flavor from this pie comes from butterscotch pudding and canned pumpkin, which work surprisingly well together. Kids go wild over the cream cheese layer!

LIZ RAISIG • NEW YORK CITY, NEW YORK

1-1/2	cups finely crushed gingersnaps (about 32 cookies)
1/4	cup butter, melted
4	ounces cream cheese, softened
1	tablespoon sugar
1-1/2	cups whipped topping
1	cup cold milk
2	packages (3.4 ounces each) instant butterscotch pudding mix
1/2	cup canned pumpkin
1/2	teaspoon pumpkin pie spice
1/2	teaspoon vanilla extract
1/4	teaspoon ground cinnamon

Additional whipped topping, optional

- In a small bowl, combine cookie crumbs and butter. Press onto the bottom and up the sides of an ungreased 9-in. pie plate. Bake at 375° for 8-10 minutes or until crust is lightly browned. Cool on a wire rack.

- For filling, in a small bowl, beat the cream cheese and sugar until smooth. Fold in whipped topping. Spread over crust.

- In a small bowl, beat the milk and pudding mixes for 1 minute. Let stand for 1-2 minutes or until soft-set. Stir in the pumpkin, pie spice, vanilla and cinnamon. Spread over the cream cheese layer. Cover and refrigerate overnight. Garnish with the additional whipped topping if desired.

YIELD: 6-8 SERVINGS.

MAKEOVER CHOCOLATE EGGNOG PIE

PREP: 45 MIN. + CHILLING

NO BAKE

I make this dessert for my family for the holidays using leftover eggnog. The delightful pie boasts all the classic flavors but half the fat and a third fewer calories, so we can savor our tradition down to the last rich crumb.

BETH MCCREEDY • LAPEER, MICHIGAN

- 1/2 cup all-purpose flour
- 1/3 cup ground walnuts
- 3 tablespoons packed brown sugar
- 1 tablespoon baking cocoa
- 1/4 cup reduced-fat butter, melted

FILLING:
- 1/2 cup sugar
- 2 tablespoons cornstarch
- 2 cups eggnog
- 2-1/2 teaspoons unflavored gelatin
- 1/2 cup cold water, divided
- 2 tablespoons baking cocoa
- 3/4 teaspoon rum extract
- 2 cups reduced-fat whipped topping

GARNISH:
- 1/2 cup reduced-fat whipped topping
- Ground nutmeg, optional

- In a bowl, combine the flour, walnuts, brown sugar and cocoa. Stir in butter. Lightly coat hands with cooking spray; press mixture into an ungreased 9-in. pie plate. Bake at 375° for 8-10 minutes or until set. Cool pie completely on a wire rack.

MAKEOVER CHOCOLATE EGGNOG PIE

- For filling, in a small saucepan, combine the sugar and cornstarch. Stir in eggnog until smooth. Bring to a boil; cook and stir for 2 minutes or until thickened and bubbly. Remove from the heat; set aside.

- Sprinkle gelatin over 1/4 cup cold water; let stand for 1 minute. Microwave on high for 20 seconds. Stir and let stand for 1 minute or until the gelatin is completely dissolved. Stir into reserved eggnog mixture.

- Divide mixture in half. Combine cocoa and remaining water; stir into one portion of eggnog mixture. Stir rum extract into the other portion. Cover and refrigerate the mixtures until partially set.

- Fold the whipped topping into the rum-flavored filling and spoon into the crust. Gently spread the chocolate filling over the top. Cover and refrigerate for at least 2 hours before serving. Garnish with the whipped topping and nutmeg.

YIELD: 8 SERVINGS.

EDITOR'S NOTE: This recipe was tested with Land O'Lakes light stick butter and commercially prepared eggnog.

CREAM CHEESE-PINEAPPLE PIE

PREP: 30 MIN. BAKE: 50 MIN.

I've made this creamy tropical pie many times for friends, relatives, guests, church suppers and bazaars, and I'm always getting requests for the recipe.

ELIZABETH BROWN • CLAYTON, DELAWARE

PINEAPPLE LAYER:
- 1/3 cup sugar
- 1 tablespoon cornstarch
- 1 can (8 ounces) crushed pineapple with juice

CREAM CHEESE LAYER:
- 1 package (8 ounces) cream cheese, softened to room temperature
- 1/2 cup sugar
- 1 teaspoon salt
- 2 eggs
- 1/2 cup milk
- 1/2 teaspoon vanilla extract
- 1 9-inch unbaked pie shell
- 1/4 cup chopped pecans

- Combine sugar, cornstarch and pineapple plus juice in a small saucepan. Cook over medium heat, stirring constantly until mixture is thick and clear. Cool; set aside. Blend cream cheese, sugar and salt in mixer bowl. Add 2 eggs, one at a time, beating well after each addition. Blend in milk and vanilla. (Mixture may look slightly curdled, but will bake out.) Spread cooled pineapple layer over bottom of pie shell. Pour cream cheese mixture over pineapple; sprinkle with pecans. Bake at 400° for 10 minutes; reduce heat to 325° and bake for 50 minutes. Cool.

YIELD: 8 SERVINGS.

PUMPKIN CHIFFON PIE

PREP: 25 MIN. + CHILLING

*This delicious pie is so light and fluffy that folks
will have room for a slice no matter how full they are!
Guests are always pleased with the delicate flavor.*

LINDA GARTNER • FEASTERVILLE, PENNSYLVANIA

1	envelope unflavored gelatin
1/2	cup cold water
3/4	cup milk
1	cup packed brown sugar
1	cup canned pumpkin
1/2	teaspoon ground ginger
1/2	teaspoon ground cinnamon
1/4	teaspoon salt
1-1/2	cups whipped topping
1	graham cracker crust (9 inches)

- In a small bowl, sprinkle gelatin over cold water; let stand for 1 minute. In a saucepan, heat milk over medium heat until bubbles form around sides of saucepan. Add gelatin mixture; stir until dissolved. Stir in brown sugar until dissolved. Remove from the heat. Add pumpkin, ginger, cinnamon and salt; mix well. Refrigerate until thickened, about 1-1/2 hours.

- Fold whipped topping into the pumpkin mixture. Pour into crust. Refrigerate for at least 4 hours or until firm. Refrigerate leftovers.

YIELD: 6-8 SERVINGS.

GERMAN CHOCOLATE PIE

PREP: 20 MIN. BAKE: 45 MIN.

*This chocolate delight has been a holiday tradition
in our family for generations, and it's just as popular
now as when my grandmother made it years ago!*

CRYSTAL ALLEN • HOMER, ILLINOIS

4	ounces German sweet chocolate, chopped
1/4	cup butter
1	can (12 ounces) evaporated milk
1-1/2	cups sugar
3	tablespoons cornstarch
1/8	teaspoon salt
2	eggs
1	teaspoon vanilla extract
1	unbaked deep-dish pie shell (9 inches)
1-1/2	cups coconut
1	cup pecans, chopped

- In a saucepan, combine the chocolate and butter. Melt over low heat. Remove from the heat and blend in milk; set aside.

PEACH CREAM PIE

- In a bowl, combine sugar, cornstarch and salt. Beat in eggs and vanilla. Blend in melted chocolate; pour into pie shell. Combine coconut and pecans; sprinkle on top of pie.

- Bake at 375° for 45 minutes.

YIELD: 8-10 SERVINGS.

PEACH CREAM PIE

PREP: 10 MIN. BAKE: 40 MIN.

*My husband and kids love this dessert and ask for it often.
It's a breeze to make and is delicious served warm or cold.*

KAREN ODOM • MELBOURNE, FLORIDA

6	medium ripe peaches, peeled and sliced
1	unbaked deep-dish pastry shell (9 inches)
1/2	cup sugar
3	tablespoons all-purpose flour
1/4	teaspoon salt
3/4	cup heavy whipping cream

- Arrange peaches in the pastry shell. In a small bowl, combine sugar, flour and salt; stir in cream until smooth. Pour over peaches.

- Bake at 400° for 40-45 minutes or until filling is almost set. Serve warm or cold. Refrigerate leftovers.

YIELD: 6-8 SERVINGS.

CARAMEL CHOCOLATE MOUSSE PIE

PREP: 30 MIN. + CHILLING

Busy cooks will love the make-ahead convenience of this no-bake pie. I prepare it the night before I'm expecting company, then garnish just before serving.

CAROL STEIG • BUTTE, NORTH DAKOTA

- 1/2 cup chopped pecans, toasted
- 1 graham cracker crust (9 inches)
- 7 ounces caramels (about 25)
- 1/4 cup evaporated milk
- 1/2 cup milk
- 20 large marshmallows
- 1 cup (6 ounces) semisweet chocolate chips
- 3 tablespoons butter, cubed
- 1 teaspoon vanilla extract
- 1 carton (8 ounces) frozen whipped topping, thawed

Additional whipped topping, toasted pecan halves and chocolate curls, optional

- Place the pecans in crust. In a heavy saucepan over medium heat, cook and stir caramels and evaporated milk until caramels are melted and mixture is smooth. Cool for 10 minutes, stirring several times. Pour over pecans; refrigerate.

- In a heavy saucepan, combine the milk, marshmallows, chocolate chips and butter; cook and stir over medium heat until marshmallows are melted and mixture is smooth. Remove from the heat; stir in vanilla. Cool to room temperature, stirring several times. Fold in whipped topping. Pour over caramel layer. Cover and refrigerate overnight. Garnish with additional whipped topping, pecans and chocolate curls if desired.

YIELD: 6-8 SERVINGS.

RASPBERRY MALLOW PIE

RASPBERRY MALLOW PIE

PREP: 35 MIN. + CHILLING

This delightful dessert features the sweet combination of marshmallows and raspberries. The recipe requires no baking and is quick-to-fix with only five ingredients. Feel free to substitute frozen strawberries if you like.

JUDIE ANGLEN • RIVERTON, WYOMING

- 35 large marshmallows
- 1/2 cup milk
- 1 package (10 ounces) sweetened frozen raspberries
- 1 carton (8 ounces) frozen whipped topping, thawed
- 1 graham cracker crust (9 inches)

- In a large microwave-safe bowl, combine marshmallows and milk. Cover and cook on high for 30-60 seconds or until marshmallows are melted; stir until smooth. Stir in raspberries. Fold in whipped topping. Pour into crust. Chill until set.

YIELD: 6-8 SERVINGS.

EDITOR'S NOTE: This recipe was tested in a 1,100-watt microwave.

VERY BERRY PIE

PREP: 15 MIN. + CHILLING

I came up with this easy pie when I needed a speedy dessert for a get-together. Everyone raved about the tangy fresh berries and smooth, white chocolate filling.

BECKY THOMPSON • MARYVILLE, TENNESSEE

- 1-3/4 cups reduced-fat whipped topping, divided
- 1 reduced-fat graham cracker crust (8 inches)
- 1 cup fresh raspberries
- 1 cup fresh blueberries

Sugar substitute equivalent to 1 tablespoon sugar

- 1 cup cold fat-free milk
- 1 package (1 ounce) sugar-free instant white chocolate pudding mix

- Spread 1/4 cup of the whipped topping into the crust. Combine the berries and sugar substitute; spoon 1 cup over topping.

- In a bowl, whisk the milk and pudding mix for 2 minutes; let stand for 2 minutes or until soft-set. Spoon over berries. Spread with remaining whipped topping. Top with remaining berries. Refrigerate for 45 minutes or until set.

YIELD: 8 SERVINGS.

EDITOR'S NOTE: This recipe was tested with Splenda no-calorie sweetener.

VERY BERRY PIE

CHOCOLATE-RASPBERRY MOUSSE PIE

CHOCOLATE-RASPBERRY MOUSSE PIE
PREP: 35 MIN. + CHILLING

(NO BAKE)

Many years ago I adapted a recipe for a raspberry mousse to make it lighter. I love the combination of the berries and chocolate in this pie.

VIRGINIA ANTHONY • JACKSONVILLE, FLORIDA

10	whole reduced-fat graham crackers
1	egg white
2	tablespoons butter, melted
1/2	cup semisweet chocolate chips
1	envelope unflavored gelatin
1/2	cup cold water
2-1/2	cups fresh raspberries
4	ounces reduced-fat cream cheese, cubed
1/2	cup sugar
1/2	cup nonfat dry milk powder
1/2	cup ice-cold water
2	tablespoons lemon juice

- Place the graham crackers in a food processor; cover and process until fine crumbs form. Add the egg white and butter; cover and process until blended. Pat onto the bottom and up the sides of a 9-in. pie plate coated with cooking spray.

- Bake at 350° for 8-10 minutes or until set. Sprinkle with chocolate chips; let stand for 1-2 minutes. Spread the melted chips over crust. Cool on a wire rack.

- In a small saucepan, sprinkle gelatin over cold water; let stand for 1 minute. Heat over low heat, stirring until gelatin is completely dissolved. Remove from the heat; set aside.

- Puree raspberries in a food processor; strain, discarding the seeds. Return puree to food processor. Add the cream cheese and sugar; cover and process until smooth. Add the gelatin mixture; cover and process until blended. Transfer to a large bowl; cover and refrigerate for 40 minutes or until partially set.

- In a small bowl, beat milk powder and ice-cold water on high speed until soft peaks form, about 7 minutes. Beat in the lemon juice. Stir a third of the mixture into raspberry mixture; fold in the remaining milk mixture. Spread evenly into crust. Cover and refrigerate for at least 3 hours.

YIELD: 8 SERVINGS.

CREAMY STRAWBERRY PIE

PREP: 25 MIN. + CHILLING

I like to end a nice meal with this easy make-ahead dessert. The eye-catching pie has a big strawberry flavor and extra richness from ice cream. It's a great cool-down on a warm summer evening.

DIXIE TERRY • GOREVILLE, ILLINOIS

- 1 package (10 ounces) frozen sweetened sliced strawberries, thawed
- 1 package (3 ounces) strawberry gelatin
- 2 cups vanilla ice cream
- 1 pastry shell (9 inches), baked

Sliced fresh strawberries, optional

- Drain the strawberries into a 1-cup measuring cup and reserve juice; set berries aside. Add enough water to juice to measure 1 cup; pour into a large saucepan. Bring to a boil over medium heat.

- Remove from the heat; stir in gelatin until dissolved. Add ice cream; stir until blended. Refrigerate for 5-10 minutes or just until thickened (watch carefully).

- Fold in the reserved strawberries. Pour into pastry shell. Refrigerate until firm, about 1 hour.

- Garnish with fresh strawberries if desired. Refrigerate leftovers.

YIELD: 6 SERVINGS.

CREAMY STRAWBERRY PIE

LEMON YOGURT CREAM PIE

LEMON YOGURT CREAM PIE

PREP: 15 MIN. + CHILLING

Creamy lemon yogurt and grated lemon peel provide the lively flavor in this tempting dessert. It's a delightful ending to a spicy or Southwestern dinner.

SUSAN KOSTECKE • ST. LOUIS, MISSOURI

- 1 envelope unflavored gelatin
- 1/4 cup cold water

Sugar substitute equivalent to 1/3 cup sugar

- 1/3 cup lemon juice
- 1-1/2 cups (12 ounces) fat-free lemon yogurt
- 1 teaspoon grated lemon peel
- 1 carton (8 ounces) frozen reduced-fat whipped topping, thawed
- 1 reduced-fat graham cracker crust (8 inches)

Lemon slice and mint, optional

- In a microwave-safe bowl, sprinkle gelatin over cold water; let stand for 1 minute. Microwave, uncovered, on high for 20 seconds. Stir in sugar substitute and lemon juice. Add yogurt and lemon peel; mix well. Fold in whipped topping; spoon into crust.

- Cover and refrigerate for 8 hours or overnight. Garnish with lemon slices and mint if desired.

YIELD: 8 SERVINGS.

EDITOR'S NOTE: This recipe was tested with Splenda no-calorie sweetener.

strawberry fans

Strawberry fans make a lovely pie garnish. Simply place a berry, stem side down, on a cutting board. With a sharp knife, make cuts, 1/8 in. apart through the berry to within 1/8 in. of the stem. Spread apart the slices to form a fan.

FLUFFY LEMON-LIME PIE

PREP: 15 MIN. + CHILLING

*You can't go wrong with this refreshing treat.
I simply mix together three ingredients, put the combination
into a prepared crust and pop it in the refrigerator.*

MRS. C.G. ROWLAND • CHATTANOOGA, TENNESSEE

- 1 envelope (.13 ounce) unsweetened lemon-lime soft drink mix
- 1 can (14 ounces) sweetened condensed milk
- 1 carton (8 ounces) frozen whipped topping, thawed
- 1 graham cracker crust (9 inches)

- In a large bowl, dissolve the soft drink mix in milk; fold in whipped topping. Spoon into the crust. Cover and refrigerate for 3 hours or until set.

YIELD: 6-8 SERVINGS.

CHOCOLATE CHERRY PIE

PREP: 15 MIN. BAKE: 15 MIN. + CHILLING

*This rich and creamy pie features the divine
blend of chocolate and cherries with
a hint of almond. One slice is never enough.*

MAXINE SMITH • OWANKA, SOUTH DAKOTA

- 1 cup all-purpose flour
- 2 tablespoons sugar
- 1/2 teaspoon salt
- 1/2 cup cold butter, cubed

FILLING:
- 1 can (14 ounces) sweetened condensed milk
- 1 cup (6 ounces) semisweet chocolate chips
- 1/2 teaspoon salt
- 1 can (21 ounces) cherry pie filling
- 1/4 to 1/2 teaspoon almond extract

Whipped cream and maraschino cherries, optional

FLUFFY LEMON-LIME PIE

- In a bowl, mix flour, sugar and salt. Cut in butter until mixture resembles coarse crumbs. Press firmly onto the bottom and sides of a 9-in. pie plate. Bake at 350° for 15-20 minutes or until golden brown. Cool completely. In a saucepan, combine the milk, chocolate chips and salt; cook and stir over low heat until chocolate melts. Stir in pie filling and extract. Pour into crust. Chill 2-3 hours or until firm. Garnish with whipped cream and cherries if desired.

YIELD: 8 SERVINGS.

LIME CREAM PIE

PREP: 20 MIN. BAKE: 15 MIN. + CHILLING

*Our home economists whipped up the recipe
for this delightfully tart and flavorful pie. The smooth texture
of the filling is similar to that of lemon meringue pie.*

TASTE OF HOME TEST KITCHEN

Pastry for single-crust pie (9 inches)
- 1-1/2 cups sugar
- 1/3 cup cornstarch
- 1/4 cup all-purpose flour
- 1/4 teaspoon salt
- 3 cups water
- 4 egg yolks, beaten
- 4-1/2 teaspoons butter
- 1-1/2 teaspoons grated lime peel

Green food coloring, optional
- 6 tablespoons lime juice

TOPPING:
- 1 cup heavy whipping cream
- 2 tablespoons sugar
- 1/2 teaspoon vanilla extract

- Line a 9-in. pie plate with pastry. Trim to 1/2 in. beyond edge of plate; flute edges. Line unpricked pastry shell with a double thickness of heavy-duty foil. Bake at 450° for 8 minutes. Remove foil; bake 5 minutes longer. Cool on a wire rack.

- For filling, in a large saucepan, combine the sugar, cornstarch, flour and salt. Stir in the water until smooth. Cook and stir over medium-high heat until thickened and bubbly. Reduce heat; cook and stir 2 minutes longer. Remove from heat.

- Stir a small amount of hot filling into yolks. Return all to pan, stirring constantly. Bring to a gentle boil; cook and stir 2 minutes longer. Remove from the heat. Stir in the butter, lime peel and food coloring if desired. Gently stir in lime juice. Pour into crust. Cool on a wire rack for 1 hour; refrigerate for at least 3 hours.

- In a small bowl, beat cream until it begins to thicken. Add the sugar and vanilla; beat until stiff peaks form. Spread or pipe topping over pie. Store in the refrigerator.

YIELD: 6-8 SERVINGS.

BANANA CREAM PIE

CHERRY CHEESE PIE
PREP: 15 MIN. + CHILLING

Preparing foods that are both low in fat and delicious can be a challenge. My health-conscious clan loves this quick, no-bake recipe, and I love that it gets me out of the kitchen so fast!

DEBBIE LUCCI • SALEM, VIRGINIA

- 2 teaspoons unflavored gelatin
- 1/4 cup cold water
- 1 package (8 ounces) reduced-fat cream cheese
- 1 teaspoon vanilla extract
- Sugar substitute equivalent to 2 tablespoons sugar
- 1 envelope whipped topping mix (Dream Whip)
- 2 cups fat-free whipped topping
- 1 reduced-fat graham cracker crust (8 inches)
- 1 cup reduced-sugar cherry pie filling

- In a small saucepan, sprinkle gelatin over cold water; let stand for 1 minute. Heat over low heat until gelatin is completely dissolved. Remove from heat; set aside.

- In a large bowl, beat cream cheese and vanilla until blended. Gradually beat in sugar substitute. Gradually add whipped topping mix; beat on medium speed for 2 minutes. Gradually beat in the gelatin mixture; beat 1 minute longer.

- Mix in 1 cup whipped topping. Fold in remaining whipped topping. Spoon into crust; top with cherry pie filling. Cover and refrigerate for at least 1 hour before serving.

YIELD: 8 SERVINGS.

EDITOR'S NOTE: This recipe was tested with Splenda no-calorie sweetener.

BANANA CREAM PIE
PREP: 20 MIN. + CHILLING

Being on a diet should not deter you from having a fantastic dessert. The light version of this classic pie tastes just as good as the original but with fewer calories and not one ounce of the guilt!

LILA CASE • BELLA VISTA, ARKANSAS

- 1-1/2 cups cold fat-free milk
- 1 package (1 ounce) sugar-free instant vanilla pudding mix
- 1/3 cup fat-free sour cream
- 1 carton (8 ounces) frozen reduced-fat whipped topping, thawed, divided
- 3 medium firm bananas, sliced
- 1 reduced-fat graham cracker crust (9 inches)

- In a bowl, whisk milk and pudding mix for 2 minutes. Let stand for 2 minutes or until soft-set. Stir in sour cream until smooth. Fold in 1-1/2 cups whipped topping.

- Place half of the banana slices in the crust; top with half of the pudding mixture. Repeat layers. Spread with the remaining whipped topping. Refrigerate for 4-6 hours before serving (pie will be soft-set). Refrigerate leftovers.

YIELD: 8 SERVINGS.

ICE CREAM & FREEZER PIES

ICE CREAM LOVERS, AND THOSE WHO LOVE A CHILLY TREAT, ARE GUARANTEED TO BE SATISFIED WITH THE FROSTY INDULGENCES ON THE PAGES THAT FOLLOW.

PEANUT BUTTER FREEZER PIE

CHOCOLATE-CHERRY ICE CREAM PIE

PREP: 15 MIN. + FREEZING

No one would ever dream that the fancy taste and look of this luscious freezer pie could come from only five simple ingredients! This makes an unbelievably easy dessert—whether for an elegant dinner party or as a cool, high-energy kids' treat on a sweltering day.

KIMBERLY WEST • PRAIRIEVILLE, LOUISIANA

- 1 bottle (7-1/4 ounces) chocolate hard-shell ice cream topping, divided
- 1 graham cracker crust (9 inches)
- 1 jar (10 ounces) maraschino cherries, drained
- 1 quart vanilla ice cream, softened
- 2 packages (1-1/2 ounces each) peanut butter cups, chopped

- Following the package directions, drizzle half of the ice cream topping over crust; gently spread to coat the bottom and sides. Freeze until firm.

- Meanwhile, set aside six cherries for garnish; chop remaining cherries. In a large bowl, combine the ice cream and chopped cherries. Spread into prepared crust. Sprinkle with the chopped peanut butter cups; drizzle with remaining ice cream topping.

- Garnish with the reserved cherries. Cover and freeze for 2 hours or until firm. Remove from the freezer 15 minutes before serving.

YIELD: 6 SERVINGS.

CHOCOLATE-CHERRY ICE CREAM PIE

FROZEN BANANA SPLIT PIE

FROZEN BANANA SPLIT PIE

PREP: 25 MIN. + FREEZING

This dessert is special enough to make hamburgers and fries a meal to remember! It's so tall and pretty and just like eating a frozen banana split. Make it ahead to save time.

JOY COLLINS • BIRMINGHAM, ALABAMA

- 3 tablespoons chocolate hard-shell ice cream topping
- 1 graham cracker crust (9 inches)
- 2 medium bananas, sliced
- 1/2 teaspoon lemon juice
- 1/2 cup pineapple ice cream topping
- 1 quart strawberry ice cream, softened
- 2 cups whipped topping
- 1/2 cup chopped walnuts, toasted
- Chocolate syrup
- 8 maraschino cherries with stems

- Pour chocolate topping into crust; freeze for 5 minutes or until chocolate is firm.

- Meanwhile, place bananas in a small bowl; toss with lemon juice. Arrange bananas over chocolate topping. Layer with the pineapple topping, ice cream, whipped topping and walnuts.

- Cover and freeze until firm. Remove from the freezer 15 minutes before cutting. Garnish with chocolate syrup and cherries.

YIELD: 8 SERVINGS.

FROSTY KEY LIME PIE

- Set aside 1/4 cup malted milk balls for topping. Place the ice cream in a large bowl; fold in the whipped topping and remaining malted milk balls. Spoon into the crust. Cover and freeze.

- Garnish with additional whipped topping if desired and reserved malted milk balls. Remove from the freezer 20 minutes before serving.

YIELD: 2 PIES (6-8 SERVINGS EACH).

CHOCOLATE ORANGE PIE

PREP: 20 MIN. + FREEZING

I dreamed up this wonderful concoction when I was yearning for the creamy orange ice cream treat of my childhood. It's a make-ahead specialty.

LAURIE LACLAIR • NORTH RICHLAND HILLS, TEXAS

1	cup miniature marshmallows
1	cup (6 ounces) semisweet chocolate chips
1	cup evaporated milk
1	pint vanilla ice cream, softened
1	pint orange sherbet, softened
1	graham cracker crust (9 inches)
1/3	cup coarsely chopped pecans

- In a saucepan, combine the marshmallows, chocolate chips and milk. Bring to a boil over medium heat; cook and stir for 2 minutes or until melted. Remove from the heat. Cool completely.

- Meanwhile, alternately arrange scoops of ice cream and sherbet in crust; smooth top. Pour chocolate sauce over pie; sprinkle with pecans. Cover and freeze for at least 4 hours. May be frozen for up to 2 months.

YIELD: 6-8 SERVINGS.

FROSTY KEY LIME PIE

PREP: 20 MIN. + FREEZING

I credit whipped cream for the fluffy-smooth texture and luscious flavor of this frozen refresher. It makes a sweet ending to a summer meal.

LISA FELD • GRAFTON, WISCONSIN

1	can (14 ounces) sweetened condensed milk
6	tablespoons key lime juice
2	cups heavy whipping cream, whipped, divided
1	graham cracker crust (9 inches)

- In a large bowl, combine the condensed milk and lime juice. Refrigerate 1/4 cup whipped cream for garnish. Fold a fourth of the remaining whipped cream into lime mixture; fold in remaining whipped cream. Spoon into crust. Cover and freeze overnight.

- Remove from the freezer 10-15 minutes before serving. Garnish with reserved whipped cream.

YIELD: 6-8 SERVINGS.

MALTED MILK PIE

PREP: 10 MIN. + FREEZING

Malted milk balls provide the delightful flavor you'll find in each cool bite of this light dessert. It's easy to assemble and a longtime favorite of my family.

JANN MARIE FOSTER • MINNEAPOLIS, MINNESOTA

1	package (7 ounces) malted milk balls, chopped
1	pint vanilla ice cream, softened
1	carton (8 ounces) frozen whipped topping, thawed
2	chocolate crumb crusts (9 inches)

Additional whipped topping, optional

CHOCOLATE ORANGE PIE

MUD PIE

MUD PIE

PREP: 25 MIN. + FREEZING

We enjoyed this cool, delicious pie while on a trip. I came home and developed my own recipe. It's always a hit!

SANDRA ASHCRAFT • PUEBLO, COLORADO

1-1/2 cups chocolate wafer crumbs
1/3 cup butter, melted
1 quart chocolate ice cream, softened
1 quart coffee ice cream, softened

CHOCOLATE SAUCE:
2 tablespoons butter
2 ounces unsweetened chocolate
1 cup sugar
1/4 teaspoon salt
1 can (5 ounces) evaporated milk
1/2 teaspoon vanilla extract

WHIPPED CREAM:
1 cup heavy whipping cream
1 tablespoon sugar

- In a small bowl, combine wafer crumbs and butter. Press onto the bottom and up the sides of an ungreased 9-in. deep-dish pie plate. Bake at 350° for 10 minutes. Cool on a wire rack.

- In a large bowl, beat chocolate ice cream and coffee ice cream. Spoon into crust. Cover and freeze for 8 hours or overnight.

- For chocolate sauce, in a small saucepan, melt butter and chocolate over low heat; stir until smooth. Stir in the sugar, salt and evaporated milk. Bring to a boil, stirring constantly. Remove from heat; stir in vanilla. Set aside.

- Remove pie from freezer 15 minutes before serving. In a small bowl, beat the cream until it begins to thicken. Gradually add sugar; beat until soft peaks form.

- Drizzle three stripes of chocolate sauce into a pastry bag; carefully add whipped cream. Pipe onto each slice of pie. Serve with remaining chocolate sauce.

YIELD: 8 SERVINGS.

CHOCOLATE ICE CREAM PIE

PREP: 15 MIN. + FREEZING

When the temperature is soaring the last thing I want to do is turn on the oven to bake dessert. Instead, I rely on fabulous freezer pies like this one.

MARGARET WILSON • HEMET, CALIFORNIA

3/4 cup small pecan halves, toasted
6 cups chocolate ice cream, softened
1/2 cup caramel ice cream topping, divided
1 graham cracker crust (9 inches)
2/3 cup whipped topping

- Set aside 12-16 pecan halves for the garnish; chop the remaining pecans. In a large bowl, combine the ice cream, 1/4 cup caramel topping and chopped pecans. Spread into pie crust. Cover; freeze for at least 2-1/2 hours.

- Remove from freezer 15 minutes before serving. Garnish with whipped topping, remaining caramel topping and reserved pecans.

YIELD: 6-8 SERVINGS.

CHOCOLATE ICE CREAM PIE

BANANA SPLIT CHEESECAKE

BANANA SPLIT CHEESECAKE

PREP: 35 MIN. + FREEZING

My fruity dessert makes a light and festive treat that's sure to dazzle friends and family at the end of any meal. I top the tempting sweet with syrup, caramel and pecans for an ooey-gooey look and mouthwatering taste.

CHERIE SWEET • EVANSVILLE, INDIANA

1   can (8 ounces) unsweetened crushed pineapple, divided
2   medium firm bananas, sliced
1   reduced-fat graham cracker crust (8 inches)
1   package (8 ounces) fat-free cream cheese
1-1/2   cups pineapple sherbet, softened
1   package (1 ounce) sugar-free instant vanilla pudding mix

1   carton (8 ounces) frozen reduced-fat whipped topping, thawed, divided
4   maraschino cherries, divided
1   tablespoon chocolate syrup
1   tablespoon caramel ice cream topping
1   tablespoon chopped pecans

● Drain the pineapple, reserving juice. In a small bowl, combine bananas and 2 tablespoons reserved juice; let stand for 5 minutes. Drain bananas, discarding juice. Arrange bananas over bottom of crust; set aside.

● In a large bowl, beat cream cheese and 2 tablespoons reserved pineapple juice. Gradually beat in sherbet. Gradually beat in pudding mix; beat 2 minutes longer. Refrigerate 1/3 cup pineapple until serving; fold remaining pineapple into cream cheese mixture. Fold in 2 cups whipped topping; spread evenly over banana slices. Cover and freeze until firm.

- Remove from the freezer 10-15 minutes before serving. Chop three maraschino cherries and pat dry; arrange cherries and reserved pineapple around edge of pie. Drizzle with the chocolate syrup and caramel topping. Dollop remaining whipped topping onto center of pie. Sprinkle with pecans; top with remaining cherry.

YIELD: 10 SERVINGS.

FROZEN
PUMPKIN MOUSSE PIE
PREP: 35 MIN. + FREEZING

Rich and creamy, this popular dessert tastes so good with its buttery graham cracker crust.

SHEILA BRADSHAW • POWELL, OHIO

1-1/2   cups graham cracker crumbs
1/4   cup packed brown sugar
6   tablespoons butter, melted
FILLING:
1   can (15 ounces) solid-pack pumpkin
1   jar (7 ounces) marshmallow creme
1/4   cup packed brown sugar
2   teaspoons pumpkin pie spice
1   carton (12 ounces) frozen whipped topping, thawed, divided

- In a bowl, combine the cracker crumbs, brown sugar and butter. Press onto the bottom and up the sides of a greased 9-in. deep-dish pie plate. Bake at 350° for 7-9 minutes or until lightly browned. Cool completely on a wire rack.

- For filling, in a large bowl, whisk pumpkin, marshmallow creme, brown sugar and the pumpkin pie spice. Fold in 3-1/2 cups whipped topping. Spoon into prepared crust. Cover; freeze for at least 4 hours or until firm. Garnish with remaining whipped topping.

YIELD: 8-10 SERVINGS.

FROZEN PUMPKIN MOUSSE PIE

BROWNIE-PEPPERMINT ICE CREAM PIE

BROWNIE-PEPPERMINT
ICE CREAM PIE
PREP: 30 MIN. BAKE: 35 MIN. + FREEZING

A rich, chocolaty brownie crust is a perfect partner to refreshing peppermint ice cream. My holiday guests have come to expect this make-ahead dessert.

CAROL GILLESPIE • CHAMBERSBURG, PENNSYLVANIA

1   package fudge brownie mix (8-inch square pan size)
1/2   cup vanilla or white chips
1/2   cup 60% cacao bittersweet chocolate baking chips
1/3   cup caramel ice cream topping
1   pint peppermint ice cream, softened
1   cup heavy whipping cream
1/4   cup confectioners' sugar
1/8   teaspoon peppermint extract
1/4   cup crushed peppermint candies

- Prepare brownie batter according to package directions; stir in the vanilla and bittersweet chips. Spread onto the bottom and up the sides of a greased 9-in. pie plate.

- Bake at 350° for 35-40 minutes or until a toothpick inserted near center comes out clean. Cool for 5 minutes. Gently press down the center of crust if necessary. Cool completely on a wire rack.

- Drizzle caramel topping over crust; spread evenly with ice cream. Cover and freeze for 4 hours or until firm.

- Remove from the freezer 10 minutes before serving. Meanwhile, in a small bowl, beat cream, confectioners' sugar and extract until stiff peaks form. Spread over ice cream; sprinkle with crushed peppermints.

YIELD: 8 SERVINGS.

FROSTY TOFFEE BITS PIE

FROSTY TOFFEE BITS PIE

PREP: 10 MIN. + FREEZING

This cool dessert tastes oh-so-good on a hot summer day or as a finale to a wonderful meal any time of year!

LADONNA REED • PONCA CITY, OKLAHOMA

- 1 package (3 ounces) cream cheese, softened
- 2 tablespoons sugar
- 1/2 cup half-and-half cream
- 1 carton (8 ounces) frozen whipped topping, thawed
- 1 package (8 ounces) milk chocolate English toffee bits, divided
- 1 graham cracker crust (9 inches)

- In a large bowl, beat cream cheese and sugar until smooth. Beat in cream until blended. Fold in whipped topping and 1 cup toffee bits.

- Spoon into the crust; sprinkle with the remaining toffee bits. Cover and freeze overnight. Remove from the freezer 10 minutes before serving.

YIELD: 6-8 SERVINGS.

softened ice cream

To soften ice cream in the fridge, transfer it to the refrigerator 20-30 minutes before using. Or let it stand at room temperature for 10-15 minutes. Hard ice cream can also be softened in the microwave at 30% power for about 30 seconds.

FROZEN COCONUT CARAMEL PIE

PREP: 20 MIN. + FREEZING

I received this recipe from a dear friend, who was a great cook and often tried new recipes. This pretty pie is just right for anyone with a sweet tooth.

LOIS TRIPLET • SPRINGHILL, LOUISIANA

- 2 tablespoons butter
- 1 cup flaked coconut
- 1/4 cup chopped pecans
- 1 package (8 ounces) cream cheese, softened
- 1 can (14 ounces) sweetened condensed milk
- 1 carton (16 ounces) frozen whipped topping, thawed
- 2 graham cracker crusts (9 inches each)
- 1 jar (12 ounces) caramel ice cream topping

- In a skillet, melt the butter; add coconut and pecans. Cook and stir over medium heat for 10 minutes or until golden brown and toasted; set aside.

- In a bowl, beat cream cheese and milk until smooth. Fold in whipped topping. Pour into crusts. Drizzle with caramel topping; sprinkle with coconut mixture.

- Cover and freeze for 8 hours or overnight or until firm. Remove from the freezer 5 minutes before slicing.

YIELD: 2 PIES (6-8 SERVINGS EACH).

CHOCOLATE-BERRY CREAM PIES

PREP: 15 MIN. + FREEZING

A chocolaty crumb crust surrounds a luscious raspberry-chocolate ice cream filling in this crowd-pleasing frozen treat. Cooks who are short on time will appreciate this recipe's use of convenience items, which keeps prep time down to a minimum.

CLEO MILLER • MANKATO, MINNESOTA

- 1/2 gallon chocolate ice cream, softened
- 1 can (11-1/2 ounces) frozen cranberry-raspberry juice concentrate, thawed
- 1 carton (16 ounces) frozen whipped topping, thawed, divided
- 3 chocolate crumb crusts (9 inches)
- 1 can (21 ounces) raspberry pie filling

- In a large bowl, combine ice cream and juice concentrate. Fold in 4 cups whipped topping. Spoon into the crusts. Cover and freeze for 4 hours or until firm.

- Remove pies from the freezer 15 minutes before serving. Garnish with pie filling and remaining whipped topping.

YIELD: 3 PIES (8 SERVINGS EACH).

CHOCOLATE-BERRY CREAM PIES

FROSTY MOCHA PIE

FROSTY MOCHA PIE
PREP: 20 MIN. + FREEZING

This pie is so rich and creamy that no one will guess it's light. The added bonus is that you can make it a day or two ahead and keep in the freezer until needed.

LISA VARNER • GREENVILLE, SOUTH CAROLINA

4	ounces reduced-fat cream cheese
1/4	cup sugar
1/4	cup baking cocoa
1	tablespoon instant coffee granules
1/3	cup fat-free milk
1	teaspoon vanilla extract
1	carton (12 ounces) frozen reduced-fat whipped topping, thawed
1	extra-servings-size graham cracker crust (9 inches)

Reduced-calorie chocolate syrup, optional

- In a large bowl, beat the cream cheese, sugar and cocoa until smooth. Dissolve coffee granules in milk. Stir coffee mixture and vanilla into cream cheese mixture; fold in whipped topping.

- Pour into the crust. Cover and freeze for at least 4 hours. Remove from freezer 10 minutes before serving. Drizzle with chocolate syrup if desired.

YIELD: 10 SERVINGS.

FREEZER PUMPKIN PIE
PREP: 20 MIN. + FREEZING

I put a cool twist on tradition with this wonderful do-ahead dessert. Gingersnaps and pecans form the delicious baked crust for the ice cream filling.

VERA REID • LARAMIE, WYOMING

1	cup ground pecans
1/2	cup finely crushed gingersnaps
1/4	cup sugar
1/4	cup butter, softened

FILLING:

1	cup canned pumpkin
1/2	cup packed brown sugar
1/2	teaspoon salt
1/2	teaspoon ground cinnamon
1/2	teaspoon ground ginger
1/4	teaspoon ground nutmeg
1	quart vanilla ice cream, slightly softened

- In a bowl, combine the pecans, gingersnaps, sugar and butter; mix well. Press into a 9-in. pie pan; bake at 450° for 5 minutes. Cool completely.

- In a bowl, beat first six filling ingredients. Stir in ice cream and mix until well blended. Spoon into crust. Freeze until firm, at least 2-3 hours. Store in freezer.

YIELD: 6-8 SERVINGS.

LEMONADE PIE WITH BLUEBERRY SAUCE

PREP: 20 MIN. + FREEZING
COOK: 5 MIN. + CHILLING

Happy endings double with this delightful, four-serving lemon pie. Enjoy half now and freeze the rest for later.

TASTE OF HOME TEST KITCHEN

2/3	cup graham cracker crumbs
4-1/2	teaspoons sugar
2	tablespoons butter, melted
2	cups vanilla ice cream, softened
1	cup whipped topping
1/2	cup thawed lemonade concentrate

SAUCE:

1	cup fresh or frozen blueberries
1/4	cup sugar
1/4	cup water, divided
1	teaspoon lemon juice
1-1/2	teaspoons cornstarch

- In a small bowl, combine the cracker crumbs and sugar; stir in butter. Press onto the bottom of a 7-in. pie plate coated with cooking spray.

- In a small bowl, combine ice cream, whipped topping and lemonade concentrate. Spread into crust; freeze for 4 hours or until firm.

- In a saucepan, combine blueberries, sugar, 2 tablespoons water and lemon juice; cook and stir over medium heat until sugar is dissolved. Combine the cornstarch and remaining water until smooth; stir into berry mixture. Bring to a boil; cook and stir for 1-2 minutes or until thickened. Refrigerate until chilled.

- Remove pie from the freezer 5 minutes before cutting. Serve with blueberry sauce.

YIELD: 4 SERVINGS (1 CUP SAUCE).

LEMONADE PIE WITH BLUEBERRY SAUCE

FROSTY CHOCOLATE PIE

FROSTY CHOCOLATE PIE

PREP: 15 MIN. + FREEZING

I turn sandwich cookies, chocolate pudding and vanilla ice cream into a dessert guaranteed to satisfy the kid in everyone. This chilled treat takes me back to my childhood because it tastes like a frozen fudge pop.

MARIA REGAKIS • SOMERVILLE, MASSACHUSETTS

15	cream-filled chocolate sandwich cookies, crushed
1/4	cup butter, melted
1	cup cold milk
1	package (3.9 ounces) instant chocolate pudding mix
2	cups vanilla ice cream, softened

Whipped topping and grated chocolate, optional

- In a large bowl, combine the cookie crumbs and butter until crumbly. Press into a greased 9-in. pie plate.

- In a large bowl, beat milk and pudding mix on low speed for 2 minutes. Fold in ice cream. Spoon into prepared crust. Cover and freeze for 4 hours or until firm.

- Remove the pie from the freezer 15 minutes before serving. Garnish with the whipped topping and the grated chocolate.

YIELD: 6-8 SERVINGS.

calling all chocolate lovers

When making a chocolate pie using a pudding mix, make it extra indulgent by tossing in a handful of semisweet or milk chocolate chips.

CHOCOLATE CHIP MALLOW PIE

PREP: 10 MIN. + FREEZING

I combine the yummy flavors of s'mores in this sweet kid-pleasing pie. I like to top each piece with just a few mini marshmallows.

JENNY BULL • HIGHLANDS RANCH, COLORADO

- 2 pints chocolate chip ice cream, softened
- 1 graham cracker crust (9 inches)
- 1 cup marshmallow creme
- 1/3 cup hot fudge ice cream topping, warmed

• Spoon ice cream into crust. Cover and freeze for at least 3 hours or until set. Remove from the freezer; spread with the marshmallow creme. Let stand for 15 minutes before cutting. Drizzle with warm fudge topping.

YIELD: 8 SERVINGS.

PEANUT BUTTER FREEZER PIE

PREP: 15 MIN. + FREEZING

It's hard to believe a pie this rich, creamy and melt-in-your-mouth delicious could be low in fat and calories.

MELISSA NEWMAN • DANVILLE, PENNSYLVANIA

- 1 package (8 ounces) fat-free cream cheese
- 3 tablespoons fat-free milk
- 2/3 cup confectioners' sugar
- 1/2 cup reduced-fat creamy peanut butter
- 1 carton (8 ounces) frozen reduced-fat whipped topping, thawed, divided
- 3/4 cup miniature semisweet chocolate chips, divided
- 1 chocolate crumb crust (8 inches)

PEANUT BUTTER FREEZER PIE

PUMPKIN ICE CREAM PIE

• In a large bowl, beat cream cheese and milk until smooth. Beat in the confectioners' sugar and peanut butter. Refrigerate 1/2 cup whipped topping for garnish. Beat 1/2 cup whipped topping into the peanut butter mixture; fold in remaining whipped topping. Set aside 8 teaspoons chocolate chips for garnish; fold remaining chips into filling.

• Spoon filling into crust. Cover and freeze for 3-4 hours or until firm. Remove from the freezer 20 minutes before serving. Garnish each slice with 1 tablespoon whipped topping and 1 teaspoon chocolate chips.

YIELD: 8 SERVINGS.

PUMPKIN ICE CREAM PIE

PREP: 15 MIN. + FREEZING

Try this quick twist on a traditional pumpkin pie. Be sure to make it ahead, so it goes from freezer to feast!

MARION STOLL • DENT, MINNESOTA

- 1 quart vanilla ice cream, softened
- 3/4 cup canned pumpkin
- 1/4 cup honey
- 1/2 teaspoon ground cinnamon
- 1/4 teaspoon salt
- 1/4 teaspoon ground ginger
- Dash ground nutmeg
- Dash ground cloves
- 1 graham cracker crust (9 inches)
- Whipped topping and pecan halves, optional

• In a large bowl, combine the first eight ingredients; beat until smooth. Spoon into crust. Cover and freeze for 2 hours or until firm.

• Remove from freezer 15 minutes before serving. Garnish with whipped topping and pecans if desired.

YIELD: 6-8 SERVINGS.

APRICOT-ALMOND ANTARCTICA

PREP: 10 MIN. + FREEZING

The combination of crunchy almonds and sweet apricots makes this chilly treat a favorite at our house.

MARCY MCREYNOLDS • NIXA, MISSOURI

1	package (12 ounces) vanilla wafers, crushed
1-1/3	cups slivered almonds, toasted
1/2	cup butter, melted
1	tablespoon almond extract
6	cups vanilla ice cream, softened
1	jar (18 ounces) apricot preserves

- In a large bowl, combine the wafer crumbs, almonds, butter and extract. Pat a third into an ungreased 13-in. x 9-in. pan. Freeze for 15 minutes.

- Carefully spread half of the ice cream over crust. Spoon half of the preserves over the ice cream. Sprinkle with half of the remaining crumb mixture. Freeze for 20-30 minutes. Repeat layers. Freeze. May be frozen for up to 2 months.

YIELD: 16-20 SERVINGS.

FROZEN PEANUT BUTTER TORTE

PREP: 35 MIN. + FREEZING

You simply can't go wrong with this frosty peanut butter torte. It's so scrumptious, and it saves time, too, as it can be made in advance.

PENNEY KESTER • SPRINGVILLE, NEW YORK

1/2	cup all-purpose flour
1/3	cup quick-cooking oats
1/4	cup sugar
1/4	cup butter, softened
1/4	teaspoon baking soda
1/2	cup crunchy peanut butter
1/3	cup light corn syrup
2	tablespoons honey
1/2	gallon vanilla ice cream, softened
3/4	cup chopped salted peanuts

- Combine first five ingredients; mix well. Pat into a greased 9-in. square baking pan. Bake at 350° for 15-17 minutes or until lightly browned. Cool to room temperature.

- Combine peanut butter, corn syrup and honey; carefully spread half over crust. Spread with half the ice cream. Drop remaining peanut butter mixture over ice cream. Sprinkle with half the nuts. Top with remaining ice cream and nuts. Freeze until firm, about 3-4 hours. Let stand 5-10 minutes before serving.

YIELD: 9-12 SERVINGS.

FROSTY COFFEE PIE

FROSTY COFFEE PIE

PREP: 15 MIN. + FREEZING

This pie was inspired by my husband, who loves coffee ice cream, and his mom, who makes a cool, creamy dessert using pudding mix.

APRIL TIMBOE • SILOAM SPRINGS, ARKANSAS

1/4	cup hot fudge ice cream topping, warmed
1	chocolate crumb crust (9 inches)
3	cups coffee ice cream, softened
1	package (5.9 ounces) instant chocolate pudding mix
1/2	cup cold strong brewed coffee
1/4	cup cold milk
1-3/4	cups whipped topping
1	cup marshmallow creme
1/4	cup miniature semisweet chocolate chips

- Spread ice cream topping into crust. In a large bowl, beat the ice cream, pudding mix, coffee and milk until blended; spoon into crust.

- In another bowl, combine the whipped topping and marshmallow creme; spread over top. Sprinkle with chocolate chips. Cover and freeze until firm.

YIELD: 8 SERVINGS.

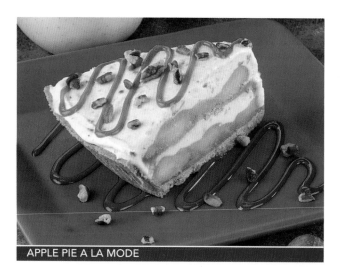

APPLE PIE A LA MODE

- In a large bowl, beat cream cheese and marshmallow creme until smooth. Stir in sherbet. Fold in whipped topping.
- Pour into the crust. Freeze until firm. Remove from the freezer 10 minutes before serving. May be frozen for up to 3 months.

YIELD: 8-10 SERVINGS.

APPLE PIE A LA MODE
PREP: 20 MIN. + FREEZING

This decadent treat combines apple pie filling and butter pecan ice cream with caramel topping and chopped nuts.

TRISHA KRUSE • EAGLE, IDAHO

1	can (21 ounces) apple pie filling
1	graham cracker crust (9 inches)
2	cups butter pecan ice cream, softened
1	jar (12 ounces) caramel ice cream topping
1/4	cup chopped pecans, toasted

- Spread half the pie filling over crust. Top with half the ice cream; cover and freeze for 30 minutes. Drizzle with half the caramel topping; cover and freeze for 30 minutes.
- Top with the remaining pie filling; cover and freeze for 30 minutes. Top with remaining ice cream; cover and freeze until firm. May be frozen for up to 2 months.
- Remove from freezer about 30 minutes before serving. Warm remaining caramel topping; drizzle some on serving plates. Top with a slice of pie; drizzle remaining caramel topping over pie and sprinkle with pecans.

YIELD: 6-8 SERVINGS.

FROSTY FREEZER PIE
PREP: 10 MIN. + FREEZING

I can whip up this pretty pie in no time! It tastes so sweet and creamy people will think you fussed. My family likes it best when I make it with orange sherbet and serve it on a warm summer day.

SUE BLOW • LITITZ, PENNSYLVANIA

1	package (8 ounces) cream cheese, softened
1	jar (7 ounces) marshmallow creme
2	cups raspberry, orange or lime sherbet, softened
2	to 3 cups whipped topping
1	graham cracker crust (9 inches)

CARAMEL TOFFEE ICE CREAM PIE
PREP: 25 MIN. + FREEZING

Try this dream of a pie when you want something easy and scrumptious. It comes together in under 30 minutes so it's ideal for entertaining.

DIANE LOMBARDO • NEW CASTLE, PENNSYLVANIA

1-1/2	cups chocolate graham cracker crumbs (about 8 whole crackers)
2	tablespoons sugar
1	egg white, beaten
2	tablespoons butter, melted
4	cups fat-free vanilla frozen yogurt, softened
2	English toffee candy bars (1.4 ounces each), coarsely chopped
1/2	cup caramel ice cream topping

- In a small bowl, combine cracker crumbs and sugar; stir in egg white and butter. Press onto the bottom and up the sides of a 9-in. pie plate coated with cooking spray. Bake at 375° for 6-8 minutes or until set. Cool completely on a wire rack.
- Spread 2-2/3 cups frozen yogurt into the crust. Sprinkle with half of the toffee bits; drizzle with half of caramel. Repeat with the remaining yogurt, toffee and caramel. Cover and freeze for 8 hours or overnight. Remove from the freezer 15 minutes before serving.

YIELD: 10 SERVINGS.

FROSTY FREEZER PIE

CARAMEL TOFFEE ICE CREAM PIE

PEANUT BUTTER CUP PIE
PREP: 25 MIN. + FREEZING

To mix things up, try different combinations of pudding mix and candy bars, such as butterscotch and Butterfingers.

TAMMY CASALETTO • GOSHEN, INDIANA

1-1/2 cups cold milk
1 package (3.9 ounces) instant chocolate pudding mix
1 cup plus 2 tablespoons coarsely chopped peanut butter cups, divided
1 carton (8 ounces) frozen whipped topping, thawed
1 chocolate crumb crust (8 or 9 inches)

- In a large bowl, whisk milk and pudding mix for 2 minutes. Let stand for 2 minutes or until soft-set. Fold in 1 cup chopped peanut butter cups. Fold in whipped topping. Spoon into crust. Cover; freeze for 6 hours or overnight.

- Remove from the freezer 15-20 minutes before serving. Garnish with the remaining chopped peanut butter cups.

YIELD: 6-8 SERVINGS.

FROZEN CRANBERRY VELVET PIE
PREP: 15 MIN. + FREEZING

This recipe is from my mother's collection. It can be made ahead, then served with ease.

MARTHA QUAM • SIOUX FALLS, SOUTH DAKOTA

1 package (8 ounces) cream cheese, softened
1 cup heavy whipping cream
1/4 cup sugar
1/2 teaspoon vanilla extract
1 can (16 ounces) whole cranberry sauce
1 pie shell (9 inches), baked

- In a bowl, beat cream cheese until fluffy. In another bowl, whip whipping cream, sugar and vanilla until thick but not stiff. Add to cream cheese, beating until smooth and creamy. Fold in cranberry sauce.

- Spoon into pie crust; freeze until firm, at least 4 hours. Remove from freezer 10 minutes before serving.

YIELD: 8-10 SERVINGS.

FROZEN GRASSHOPPER TORTE
PREP: 25 MIN. + FREEZING

I first made this tasty torte for a ladies' meeting at our church, and it went over very well. I've made it often since then and have received many compliments from young and old alike.

ELMA PENNER • OAK BLUFF, MANITOBA

4 cups crushed cream-filled chocolate cookies (about 40)
1/4 cup butter, melted
1 pint vanilla ice cream, softened
1/4 cup milk
1 jar (7 ounces) marshmallow creme
1/4 to 1/2 teaspoon peppermint extract
Few drops green food coloring
2 cups heavy whipping cream, whipped

- Combine cookie crumbs and butter. Set aside 1/4 cup for garnish; press remaining crumbs onto the bottom of a 9-in. springform pan, two 9-in. pie plates or a 13-in. x 9-in. dish. Chill for 30 minutes. Spread ice cream over crust. Freeze.

FROZEN GRASSHOPPER TORTE

S'MORE ICE CREAM PIE

STRAWBERRY BANANA PIE

PREP: 45 MIN. + FREEZING

With its sugar cone crust and layers of bananas and strawberry ice cream, this pretty pie never seems to last long...especially when our grandchildren visit. It's a favorite year–round, but we really enjoy it in summer when fresh strawberries are plentiful.

BERNICE JANOWSKI • STEVENS POINT, WISCONSIN

1	package (5-1/4 ounces) ice cream sugar cones, crushed
1/4	cup ground pecans
1/3	cup butter, melted
2	cups vanilla ice cream, softened
2	medium ripe bananas, mashed
2	large firm bananas, cut into 1/4-inch slices
2	cups strawberry ice cream, softened
1	pint fresh strawberries
1	carton (8 ounces) frozen whipped topping, thawed

- In a large bowl, combine the crushed ice cream cones, pecans and butter. Press onto the bottom and up the sides of a greased 10-in. pie plate. Refrigerate for at least 30 minutes.

- In another large bowl, combine vanilla ice cream and mashed bananas. Spread over the crust; cover and freeze for 30 minutes.

- Arrange sliced bananas over ice cream; cover and freeze for 30 minutes.

- Top with strawberry ice cream; cover and freeze for about 45 minutes.

- Hull and halve strawberries; place around edge of pie. Mound or pipe the whipped topping in center of pie. Cover and freeze for up to 1 month. Remove from the freezer about 30 minutes before serving.

YIELD: 8-10 SERVINGS.

- In a small bowl, combine milk and marshmallow creme; stir until well blended. Add extract and food coloring. Fold in whipped cream. Spoon over the ice cream and sprinkle with reserved crumbs. Freeze until firm.

YIELD: 12-16 SERVINGS.

S'MORE ICE CREAM PIE

PREP: 20 MIN. + FREEZING

Looking for the next best thing to that classic campfire treat? Try this easy and elegant freezer pie from our home economists. It melts in your mouth!

TASTE OF HOME TEST KITCHEN

2/3	cup graham cracker crumbs
2	tablespoons sugar
3	tablespoons butter, melted
2-1/2	cups rocky road ice cream, softened
2/3	cup marshmallow creme
3/4	cup miniature marshmallows

- In a small bowl, combine the cracker crumbs and sugar; stir in butter. Press onto the bottom and up the sides of a 7-in. pie plate coated with cooking spray. Bake at 325° for 7-9 minutes or until lightly browned. Cool on a wire rack.

- Carefully spread ice cream into crust; freeze until firm. Spread marshmallow creme over ice cream. Top with marshmallows; gently press into creme. Cover and freeze for 4 hours or overnight.

- Just before serving, broil 6 in. from the heat for 1-2 minutes or until marshmallows are golden brown.

YIELD: 4 SERVINGS.

STRAWBERRY BANANA PIE

FROZEN LEMON PIE

NO-CRUST TROPICAL PIE
PREP: 20 MIN. + FREEZING

*I'm a busy mom so I appreciate freezer dishes
that don't take away from family time in the evening. These
creamy coconut wedges are a frequent request at my house.*

KIM RIDGEWAY • OKEECHOBEE, FLORIDA

1	package (8 ounces) cream cheese, softened
1/3	cup sugar
1/2	teaspoon rum extract
1	can (8 ounces) crushed pineapple, undrained
2-1/3	cups flaked coconut, divided
1	carton (8 ounces) frozen whipped topping, thawed, divided

- In a large bowl, beat the cream cheese, sugar and extract until smooth. Fold in the pineapple, 2 cups coconut and 2 cups whipped topping. Pour into an ungreased 9-in. pie plate. Top with remaining whipped topping.
- Toast the remaining coconut and sprinkle over the top. Cover and freeze for at least 3 hours before cutting. May be frozen up to 3 months.

YIELD: 6-8 SERVINGS.

FROZEN LEMON PIE
PREP: 25 MIN. + FREEZING

*This refreshing dessert is simple to whip up and serve.
I like to treat my clan to this pie as a fitting finale to
a grilled meal on a warm summer evening.*

DAI SMITH • YORK, NEBRASKA

3/4	cup graham cracker crumbs (about 12 squares)
2	tablespoons plus 2 teaspoons butter, melted
2	tablespoons sugar

FILLING:

1/3	cup thawed lemonade concentrate
2	drops yellow food coloring, optional
1	cup vanilla ice cream, softened
1-3/4	cups whipped topping

Grated lemon peel, optional

mix it up
Create exciting flavor twists in recipes like Frozen Lemon Pie or Frozen Orange Cream Pie. Feel free to substitute pink lemonade concentrate using red food coloring or limeade concentrate using green coloring.

- In a bowl, combine the cracker crumbs, butter and sugar. Press onto the bottom and 1 in. up the sides of a greased 6-in. springform pan. Bake at 375° for 6-8 minutes or until the crust is lightly browned. Cool crust completely on a wire rack.
- For filling, in a bowl, beat lemonade concentrate and food coloring if desired for 30 seconds. Gradually spoon in ice cream and blend. Fold in whipped topping. Spoon into prepared crust. Freeze until solid, about 2 hours.
- Remove from the freezer 10-15 minutes before serving. Garnish with lemon peel if desired.

YIELD: 6 SERVINGS.

FROZEN ORANGE CREAM PIE
PREP: 5 MIN. + FREEZING

*Dessert doesn't get much easier than this frosty
five-ingredient favorite. It's so cool and refreshing, and
kids like it because it tastes like a frozen orange cream pop.*

NANCY HORSBURGH • EVERETT, ONTARIO

2-1/2	cups vanilla ice cream, softened
1	cup thawed orange juice concentrate
3	drops red food coloring, optional
1	drop yellow food coloring, optional
1	graham cracker crust (9 inches)

- In a bowl, combine ice cream and orange juice concentrate. Stir in food coloring if desired. Spoon into crust. Cover and freeze for 8 hours or overnight. Remove from the freezer 10 minutes before serving.

YIELD: 6-8 SERVINGS.

FROZEN ORANGE CREAM PIE

TARTS & DESSERT PIZZAS

SOMETIMES THE BEST THINGS COME IN SMALL PACKAGES. HERE YOU'LL FIND A SWEET ARRAY OF PETITE TARTS AND YUMMY DESSERT PIZZAS, MANY OF WHICH DON'T REQUIRE MUCH EFFORT.

GINGERED STRAWBERRY TART

CRANBERRY CHEESECAKE TARTLETS (NO BAKE)

PREP: 35 MIN. + CHILLING

*Ordinary cranberry sauce becomes extraordinary
when spooned on top of a cheesecake filling inside a
nutty crust. This is a great make-ahead recipe.*

TASTE OF HOME TEST KITCHEN

- 1 cup slivered almonds, toasted
- 1/4 cup all-purpose flour
- 3 tablespoons sugar
- 1/4 cup cold butter, cubed
- 2 packages (3 ounces each) cream cheese, softened
- 1/4 cup confectioners' sugar
- 2 tablespoons lemon juice
- 1 cup whipped topping
- 1 cup whole-berry cranberry sauce

- In a food processor, combine the almonds, flour and sugar; cover and process until blended. Add the butter; cover and process until mixture forms coarse crumbs.

- Press onto the bottom and up sides of four greased 4-in. tart pans with removable bottoms. Bake at 350° for 13-15 minutes or until golden brown. Cool completely on a wire rack.

- In a small bowl, beat cream cheese until smooth. Add confectioners' sugar and lemon juice until smooth and mix well. Fold in whipped topping.

- Spoon into crusts. Cover and refrigerate for 4 hours or until set. Just before serving, top with cranberry sauce.

YIELD: 4 SERVINGS.

CRANBERRY CHEESECAKE TARTLETS

SUGAR COOKIE FRUIT PIZZA

SUGAR COOKIE FRUIT PIZZA

PREP: 30 MIN. + CHILLING

*Here's my family's favorite fruit pizza. I make it
whenever we crave a cool, delicious dessert.*

GAYNELLE HENRY • NEWLAND, NORTH CAROLINA

- 1 tube (16-1/2 ounces) refrigerated sugar cookie dough
- 1 cup sugar, divided
- 2 tablespoons cornstarch
- 1/2 cup orange juice
- 1/4 cup lemon juice
- 1 package (8 ounces) cream cheese, softened
- 1 tablespoon milk
- 1 teaspoon grated orange peel
- 2/3 cup heavy whipping cream
- 1-1/2 cups halved fresh strawberries
- 1 medium peach, thinly sliced
- 1 small banana, sliced
- 1 small apple, thinly sliced
- 1/2 cup fresh blueberries

- Let dough stand at room temperature for 5-10 minutes to soften. Press onto an ungreased 14-in. pizza pan. Bake at 350° for 15-18 minutes or until deep golden brown. Cool on a wire rack.

- In a small saucepan, combine 1/2 cup sugar, cornstarch and juices. Bring to a boil; cook and stir for 2 minutes or until thickened. Remove from heat; set aside to cool.

- In a large bowl, beat the cream cheese, milk, orange peel and remaining sugar until blended.

- In a small bowl, beat cream until soft peaks form; fold into cream cheese mixture. Spread over crust. Arrange fruit over filling; spread with reserved glaze. Refrigerate until chilled.

YIELD: 12 SERVINGS.

- Referring to the photo for position, arrange five rows of strawberries on top of the pizza to create the red strips of flag. Place the blueberries in the upper left corner.

- Cut a hole in the corner of the plastic or pastry bag and insert the star tip. Fill the bag with the reserved cream cheese mixture. For the white stripes, pipe a zigzag pattern between the rows of strawberries.

- Canadian flag: In a bowl, beat the cream cheese and sugar. Add the vanilla and lemon juice, mixing until smooth. Spread 3/4 cup cream cheese mixture over the crust. Set the remaining mixture aside.

- Arrange strawberries in the shape of a maple leaf on top of the pizza.

- Cut a hole in the corner of the plastic or pastry bag and insert the round tip. Fill the bag with the reserved cream cheese mixture. Pipe veins on the maple leaf.

YIELD: 1 PIZZA.

PATRIOTIC PIZZAS

PREP/TOTAL TIME: 30 MIN. + COOLING

Here's a pie-in-the-sky idea: a dessert pizza you decorate like a high-flyin' flag!

TASTE OF HOME TEST KITCHEN

CRUST:
- 1   cup all-purpose flour
- 1/2 cup confectioners' sugar
- 1/2 cup cold butter

AMERICAN FLAG:
- 2   packages (8 ounces each) cream cheese, softened
- 1   cup sugar
- 1   teaspoon vanilla extract
- 1/2 teaspoon lemon juice
- 2   cups halved fresh strawberries
- 1/2 cup fresh or frozen blueberries

Star pastry tip #21

CANADIAN FLAG:
- 1   package (8 ounces) cream cheese, softened
- 1/2 cup sugar
- 1/2 teaspoon vanilla extract
- 1/4 teaspoon lemon juice
- 3   cups halved fresh strawberries

Round pastry tip #5

- Pizza crust: In a bowl, combine flour and confectioners' sugar. Cut the butter into dry ingredients until crumbly. Press the mixture onto a greased 12-in. pizza pan. Bake at 325° for 10-15 minutes or until the crust is lightly browned. Let cool.

- American flag: In a bowl, beat the cream cheese and sugar. Add the vanilla and lemon juice, mixing until smooth. Spread 1 cup cream cheese mixture over the crust. Set the remaining cream cheese mixture aside.

FLUFFY COCOA TARTS

PREP/TOTAL TIME: 15 MIN.

You can't go wrong with these cute tarts and their chocolaty whipped filling. They're so yummy you'll be tempted to indulge in an extra serving! This recipe is as easy as it is delicious.

TINA WOOTEN • BRANDON, FLORIDA

- 2   ounces cream cheese, softened
- 1/4   cup sour cream
- 3   tablespoons sugar
- 1/4   teaspoon lemon juice
- 4-1/2 teaspoons instant hot cocoa mix
- 3/4   cup whipped topping
- 3   individual graham cracker tart shells
- 2   teaspoons chopped salted peanuts
- 2   teaspoons miniature semisweet chocolate chips

RASPBERRY CREAM TARTS

- In a small bowl, combine the cream cheese, sour cream, sugar and lemon juice until smooth. Stir in cocoa mix. Fold in whipped topping.

- Spoon into the tart shells. Sprinkle with peanuts and chocolate chips. Cover and refrigerate until serving.

YIELD: 3 SERVINGS.

RASPBERRY CREAM TARTS

PREP/TOTAL TIME: 45 MIN. + CHILLING

I top a shortbread cookie shell with almond filling and fresh berries to create this appealing dessert that's perfect for two.

DANA DZIEDZIC • DAGGETT, MICHIGAN

1	teaspoon unflavored gelatin
1/2	cup cold 2% milk, divided
4	teaspoons sugar
1	tablespoon all-purpose flour

Dash salt

1	egg yolk, lightly beaten
1/4	teaspoon almond extract

CRUST:

1/2	cup all-purpose flour
2	tablespoons sugar
1/8	teaspoon salt
3	tablespoons butter, softened

1/3	cup heavy whipping cream
4	teaspoons confectioners' sugar
3/4	cup fresh raspberries

- In a small wide-bottom bowl, sprinkle the gelatin over 1 tablespoon milk; let stand for 2 minutes. In a small saucepan, combine sugar, flour and salt. Gradually whisk in remaining milk until smooth. Cook and stir over medium-high heat until thickened and bubbly. Reduce heat; cook and stir 2 minutes longer. Remove from heat.

- Stir a small amount of hot filling into egg yolk; return all to the pan, stirring constantly. Bring to a gentle boil; cook and stir 2 minutes longer. Remove from the heat. Stir a small amount of hot liquid into gelatin mixture. Stir until gelatin is dissolved; return to pan. Gently stir in extract. Cover and cool to room temperature without stirring, about 30 minutes.

- For crust, in a small bowl, combine flour, sugar and salt; blend in butter with a wooden spoon until smooth. Press onto the bottom and up the sides of two 4-in. tart pans with removable bottoms coated with cooking spray.

- Bake at 375° for 12-15 minutes or until golden brown. Cool on a wire rack.

- In a small bowl, beat cream until it begins to thicken. Add confectioners' sugar; beat until soft peaks form. Fold into filling mixture. Spoon into tart shells. Cover and chill for at least 1 hour. Top with raspberries.

YIELD: 2 SERVINGS.

LEMON TART
WITH ALMOND CRUST
PREP: 40 MIN. BAKE: 10 MIN. + COOLING

Our state produces an abundance of lemons, and everyone is always looking for new ways to use them. This beautiful tart is my delectible solution to the excess-lemon problem!

LOIS KINNEBERG ● PHOENIX, ARIZONA

1	cup all-purpose flour
1/2	cup sliced almonds, toasted
1/4	cup sugar
6	tablespoons cold butter
1/2	teaspoon almond extract
1/4	teaspoon salt
2	to 3 tablespoons cold water

FILLING:

3	eggs
3	egg yolks
1	cup sugar
3/4	cup lemon juice
2	tablespoons grated lemon peel

Dash salt

6	tablespoons butter, cubed

- Place flour, almonds, sugar, butter, extract and salt in a food processor. Cover and pulse until blended. Gradually add water, 1 tablespoon at a time, pulsing until mixture forms a soft dough.

- Press onto the bottom and up the sides of a greased 9-in. fluted tart pan with a removable bottom. Bake at 400° for 15-20 minutes or until golden brown. Cool on a wire rack.

- In a small heavy saucepan over medium heat, whisk the eggs, egg yolks, sugar, lemon juice, peel and salt until blended. Add butter; cook, whisking constantly, until mixture is thickened and coats the back of a metal spoon. Pour into crust. Bake at 325° for 8-10 minutes or until set. Cool on a wire rack. Refrigerate leftovers.

YIELD: 6-8 SERVINGS.

LEMON TART WITH ALMOND CRUST

FRUIT PIZZA

FRUIT PIZZA

PREP/TOTAL TIME: 40 MIN. + COOLING

This delicious recipe allows you to make use of the fresh fruits available during the summer, even as far north as Wisconsin! It's colorful and great for dessert or brunch.

DORIS SATHER ● STRUM, WISCONSIN

CRUST:

1/2	cup butter, softened
1/2	cup shortening
1	cup sugar
1	egg
1	teaspoon vanilla extract
2	cups all-purpose flour
1/2	teaspoon cream of tartar
1/2	teaspoon baking soda
1/4	teaspoon salt

CREAM FILLING:

2	packages (8 ounces each) cream cheese, softened
1	cup confectioners' sugar
1	carton (8 ounces) frozen whipped topping, thawed

GLAZE:

2	tablespoons cornstarch
1	cup pineapple juice
1	cup orange juice
1-1/2	cups fresh raspberries
2	kiwifruit, peeled and sliced
2	medium bananas, sliced
1	pint fresh strawberries, hulled and sliced

- In a small bowl, cream the butter, shortening and sugar until light and fluffy. Add egg and vanilla. Combine the dry ingredients; gradually add to the creamed mixture. Press dough into a 14- or 16-in. pizza pan. Bake at 350° 8-10 minutes or until light golden brown. Cool.

- For filling, beat cream cheese until smooth; add sugar and whipped topping. Spread over crust.

- For glaze, in a small saucepan, combine the cornstarch and juices until smooth. Bring to a boil. Cook and stir for 1-2 minutes until thickened. Set aside 1/2 cup; spread remaining warm glaze over filling.

- Arrange fruit over pizza; brush with reserved glaze. Chill until serving. (Note: If making a day ahead, substitute another seasonal fruit for bananas.)

YIELD: 12 SERVINGS.

GINGERED STRAWBERRY TART

CHOCOLATE PUDDING PIZZA
PREP: 35 MIN. + CHILLING

My sister and I came up with this easy recipe. Our family loves the classic pairing of chocolate and peanut butter presented in this whole new way.

LADONNA REED • PONCA CITY, OKLAHOMA

1	package (17-1/2 ounces) peanut butter cookie mix
1	carton (12 ounces) softened cream cheese
1-3/4	cups cold milk
1	package (3.9 ounces) instant chocolate pudding mix
1	carton (8 ounces) frozen whipped topping, thawed
1/4	cup miniature semisweet chocolate chips

- Prepare the cookie mix dough according to package directions. Press into a greased 12-in. pizza pan. Bake at 375° for 15 minutes or until set; cool.

- In a bowl, beat cream cheese until smooth. Spread over crust. In another bowl, beat milk and pudding mix on medium speed for 2 minutes. Spread over the cream cheese layer. Refrigerate for 20 minutes or until set. Spread with whipped topping. Sprinkle with chips. Chill for 1-2 hours.

YIELD: 12 SERVINGS.

CHOCOLATE PUDDING PIZZA

GINGERED STRAWBERRY TART
PREP: 35 MIN. + CHILLING

This strawberry delight is wonderful with or without the crystallized ginger. It looks elegant and tastes great, too.

MARIE RIZZIO • INTERLOCHEN, MICHIGAN

24	gingersnap cookies (about 1 cup)
2	tablespoons plus 1/3 cup sugar, divided
1/4	cup butter, melted
2	tablespoons cornstarch
1	teaspoon finely chopped crystallized ginger, optional
3	cups chopped fresh strawberries
1/4	cup water

TOPPING:

2	cups sliced fresh strawberries
5	tablespoons seedless strawberry jam

- In a food processor, combine gingersnaps, 2 tablespoons sugar and butter. Cover and process until blended. Press onto the bottom and up the sides of a 9-in. fluted tart pan with a removable bottom; set aside.

- In a large saucepan, combine the cornstarch, ginger if desired and remaining sugar. Stir in chopped strawberries and water. Bring to a boil; cook and stir for 2 minutes. Reduce the heat; simmer, uncovered, for 4-6 minutes or until thickened. Cool for 30 minutes. Pour into crust. Cover and refrigerate 2 hours or until set.

- Arrange sliced berries over filling. In a small microwave-safe bowl, heat jam on high for 15-20 seconds or until pourable; brush over berries.

YIELD: 8 SERVINGS.

CARAMELIZED APPLE TARTS

CARAMELIZED APPLE TARTS
PREP/TOTAL TIME: 45 MIN. + COOLING

This recipe cleverly dresses up frozen puff pastry and a no-bake cheesecake mix. Guests will be delighted to be offered their own individual tarts.

TASTE OF HOME TEST KITCHEN

- 1 package (17.3 ounces) frozen puff pastry, thawed
- 1 package (11.1 ounces) no-bake cheesecake mix
- 1/2 cup butter, cubed
- 1 cup packed dark brown sugar
- 1/2 teaspoon ground cinnamon
- 5 medium apples, peeled and thinly sliced
- 3 tablespoons heavy whipping cream

- Unfold pastry sheets on a lightly floured surface. Cut into eight 4-in. circles. Place on greased baking sheets. Bake at 400° for 15-18 minutes or until lightly browned. Remove to wire racks to cool.

- Prepare the cheesecake filling according to package directions; set aside. (Save the packet of crust crumbs for another use.)

- In a large skillet, melt the butter and brown sugar over medium heat; stir in cinnamon. Add half of the apples; cook and stir for 10 minutes or until tender.

- Remove with a slotted spoon to a bowl. Repeat with the remaining apples. Drain the cooking juices, reserving 1/3 cup in the skillet; discard remaining juices. Add cream to skillet; cook and stir for 2 minutes.

- Split each pastry in half horizontally. Top each with 2 heaping tablespoons of cheesecake filling. Top with apple slices and drizzle with caramel sauce. Refrigerate any leftovers.

YIELD: 16 SERVINGS.

CHOCOLATE CARAMEL TART
PREP: 35 MIN. + CHILLING

Look no further when you want a dessert that's gooey and good! Each piece is like a big candy bar on a plate.

MARGARET PETERSON • FOREST CITY, IOWA

- 2 cups crushed chocolate wafers (about 35 wafers)
- 1/3 cup butter, melted
- 30 caramels
- 1/2 cup caramel ice cream topping
- 1/2 cup heavy whipping cream, divided
- 2 cups chopped pecans
- 3/4 cup semisweet chocolate chips

- In a small bowl, combine the wafer crumbs and butter; press onto the bottom of a greased 9-in. springform pan. Place pan on a baking sheet. Bake at 350° for 10 minutes. Cool on a wire rack.

- In a heavy saucepan, cook and stir the caramels and caramel topping over low heat until smooth. Remove from the heat; stir in 1/4 cup cream and pecans. Spread over crust. Cover and refrigerate for 1 hour.

- In a saucepan, melt chocolate chips with remaining cream over low heat, stirring until smooth. Drizzle over tart. Cover and refrigerate for 1 hour or until serving.

YIELD: 12 SERVINGS.

CHOCOLATE CARAMEL TART

TANGY LEMON-NUT TART

TANGY LEMON-NUT TART
PREP: 15 MIN. **BAKE:** 20 MIN. + COOLING

*If you love traditional lemon bars, you won't be able
to resist this tangy tart with a coconut twist. I like to
top wedges with whipped cream or ice cream.
Refrigerated crescent rolls keep prep easy.*

MARY DETWEILER • MIDDLEFIELD, OHIO

- 1 tube (8 ounces) refrigerated crescent rolls
- 4 eggs
- 1 cup sugar
- 2 tablespoons all-purpose flour
- 4 teaspoons lemon juice
- 1 tablespoon grated lemon peel
- 1 cup flaked coconut
- 1/2 cup chopped blanched almonds, hazelnuts or walnuts

Confectioners' sugar

- Separate crescent dough into eight triangles; place in an 11-in. fluted tart pan with a removable bottom with points toward the center. Press dough onto the bottom and up the sides of pan to form a crust; seal perforations. Bake at 350° for 5 minutes.

- Meanwhile, in a small bowl, beat the eggs, sugar, flour, lemon juice and peel until blended. Stir in the coconut and nuts.

- Pour over the hot crust. Bake for 20-25 minutes or until lightly browned. Cool on a wire rack. Sprinkle with the confectioners' sugar. Refrigerate leftovers.

YIELD: 8 SERVINGS.

lemon juice
When a recipe calls for juice from a
fresh lemon, you can use either fresh,
frozen or bottled lemon juice in equal
amounts. Whenever you have excess
lemons on hand, juice them and
freeze the juice in ice cube trays.

ROCKY ROAD PIZZA
PREP/TOTAL TIME: 20 MIN.

*Looking for a new, interesting dessert to offer your
hungry clan? Chocolate lovers will relish this palate-pleasing
pizza that cleverly captures the flavor of rocky road
ice cream. Folks will have a hard time eating just one slice!*

TASTE OF HOME TEST KITCHEN

Pastry for single-crust pie (9 inches)
- 3/4 cup semisweet chocolate chips
- 1/2 cup miniature marshmallows
- 1/4 cup salted peanuts

- On a lightly floured surface, roll the pastry into a 9-in. circle; place on a lightly greased baking sheet. Prick with a fork. Bake at 450° for 8-10 minutes or until lightly browned. Sprinkle with chocolate chips. Bake 1-2 minutes longer or until chocolate is softened.

- Spread chocolate over crust to within 1/2 in. of edges. Sprinkle with marshmallows. Bake for 1-2 minutes or until marshmallows puff slightly and are lightly browned. Sprinkle with peanuts. Remove to a wire rack to cool.

YIELD: 6-8 SLICES.

ROCKY ROAD PIZZA

RUSTIC PEAR TART

PREP: 25 MIN. BAKE: 45 MIN. + COOLING

The pastry makes a "pouch" for a pleasant pear filling in this delight. For even more flavor, top the tart with a powdered sugar glaze and toasted almonds.

TASTE OF HOME TEST KITCHEN

1-1/3	cups all-purpose flour
3	tablespoons sugar
1/4	teaspoon salt
7	tablespoons cold butter, cubed
2	to 3 tablespoons cold water

FILLING:

3/4	cup sugar
1/4	cup slivered almonds, toasted
1/4	cup all-purpose flour
1-1/2	teaspoons dried grated lemon peel
1/2	to 3/4 teaspoon ground cinnamon
4	medium ripe pears, peeled and sliced
1	tablespoon butter

TOPPING:

1	egg white
1	teaspoon water
1	tablespoon coarse sugar

GLAZE (optional):

1/4	cup confectioners' sugar
1-1/2	teaspoons milk
1/4	teaspoon vanilla extract
1/4	cup slivered almonds, toasted

- In a small bowl, combine the flour, sugar and salt; cut in butter until crumbly. Gradually add water, tossing with a fork until dough forms a ball. Roll out to a 14-in. circle. Transfer pastry to a 14-in. pizza pan.

- In a large bowl, combine the sugar, almonds, flour, lemon peel and cinnamon. Add pears; toss to coat. Spoon over the pastry to within 2 in. of edges; dot with butter. Fold edges of pastry over pears.

- For topping, beat the egg white and water. Brush over pastry; sprinkle with the coarse sugar. Bake at 375° for 45-50 minutes or until golden brown.

RUSTIC PEAR TART

CRANBERRY CHEESECAKE TART

- For glaze, combine the confectioners' sugar, milk and vanilla. Pour over warm tart. Sprinkle with almonds. Cool on a wire rack. Store in the refrigerator.

YIELD: 10 SERVINGS.

CRANBERRY CHEESECAKE TART

PREP: 35 MIN. + CHILLING

I created this cranberry tart recipe to reduce the sugar and fat found in its higher-calorie counterpart. My light version calls for sugar substitute and reduced-fat ingredients, but tastes just as wonderful as the original!

DIANE HALFERTY • CORPUS CHRISTI, TEXAS

	Pastry for single-crust pie (9 inches)
1/3	cup sugar
2	tablespoons cornstarch
2/3	cup water
3	cups fresh or frozen cranberries
	Sugar substitute equivalent to 1 tablespoon sugar
1	package (8 ounces) reduced-fat cream cheese
1-1/2	cups reduced-fat whipped topping, divided
1	teaspoon grated lemon peel

- Press pastry onto bottom and up sides of a 10-in. tart pan with removable bottom. Bake at 400° for 9-11 minutes or until lightly browned. Cool on a wire rack.

- In a large saucepan, combine the sugar, cornstarch and water until smooth. Add cranberries. Bring to a boil over medium heat. Reduce the heat to low; cook and stir for 3-5 minutes or until thickened and berries have popped. Remove from the heat; cool to room temperature. Stir in the sugar substitute.

- In a small bowl, beat the cream cheese and 1 cup whipped topping until smooth; add the lemon peel. Spread over the pastry; top with the cranberry mixture. Refrigerate for 2-4 hours or until set. Garnish with the remaining whipped topping.

YIELD: 10 SERVINGS.

EDITOR'S NOTE: This recipe was tested with Splenda no-calorie sweetener.

STAR-SPANGLED FRUIT TART

STAR-SPANGLED FRUIT TART

PREP/TOTAL TIME: 35 MIN. + COOLING

This dessert is perfect for a Fourth of July celebration. With patriotic colors and a creamy filling, it will be the hit of the party!

RENAE MONCUR • BURLEY, IDAHO

RENAE MONCUR • BURLEY, IDAHO

1	tube (18 ounces) refrigerated sugar cookie dough, softened
1	package (8 ounces) cream cheese, softened
1/4	cup sugar
1/2	teaspoon almond extract
1	cup fresh blueberries
1	cup fresh raspberries
1	cup halved fresh strawberries

- Press cookie dough onto an ungreased 12-in. pizza pan. Bake at 350° for 10-15 minutes or until golden brown. Cool on a wire rack.

- In a small bowl, beat the cream cheese, sugar and extract until smooth. Spread over the crust. In the center of tart, arrange berries in the shape of a star; add a berry border. Refrigerate until serving.

YIELD: 16 SERVINGS.

STRAWBERRY SWIRL MOUSSE TARTS

PREP: 10 MIN. + CHILLING

Looking for a no-bake treat you can whip up in a jiffy? Try this special six-ingredient dessert from our home economists. The white chocolate and strawberry combination is absolutely too luscious to resist.

TASTE OF HOME TEST KITCHEN

1-1/2	cups cold milk
1	package (3.3 ounces) instant white chocolate pudding mix
1	cup whipped topping
1	package (6 count) individual graham cracker tart shells
1/4	cup strawberry ice cream topping
6	fresh strawberries

- In a small bowl, gradually whisk the milk and pudding for 2 minutes. Let stand for 2 minutes or until soft-set. Gently fold in whipped topping. Spoon into tart shells. Drizzle with strawberry topping. Refrigerate for at least 30 minutes. Garnish with strawberries.

YIELD: 6 SERVINGS.

CRUNCHY PEANUT BUTTER TARTS

PREP: 10 MIN. + CHILLING

Try these darling tarts for a fun, fuss-free dessert.
They are so simple to make and a rich,
satisfying way to get your peanut butter fix.

MARY KELLEY ● WILMINGTON, NORTH CAROLINA

2	ounces cream cheese, softened
1/4	cup chunky peanut butter
2	tablespoons sugar
2	tablespoons sour cream
1/4	teaspoon vanilla extract
2	individual graham cracker tart shells
2	tablespoons whipped topping

Chopped peanuts, optional

● In a small bowl, beat the cream cheese, peanut butter and sugar until blended. Stir in sour cream and vanilla. Spoon into tart shells. Refrigerate tarts for at least 1 hour. Top with the whipped topping. Sprinkle with the peanuts if desired.

YIELD: 2 SERVINGS.

STRAWBERRY TART

STRAWBERRY TART

PRE/TOTAL TIME: 30 MIN. + CHILLING

Looking for the perfect ending to any
summertime meal? Here's a swift-to-fix tart that boasts
a surprise chocolate layer beneath fluffy cream cheese.

DAWN TRINGALI ● HAMILTON SQUARE, NEW JERSEY

1	sheet refrigerated pie pastry
3	ounces German sweet chocolate, melted
2	packages (8 ounces each) cream cheese, softened
3	tablespoons heavy whipping cream
2	teaspoons vanilla extract
1-3/4	cups confectioners' sugar
2-1/2	cups sliced fresh strawberries
1/4	cup red currant jelly

● Press pastry onto the bottom and up the sides of an ungreased 9-in. fluted tart pan with a removable bottom. Place on a baking sheet. Bake at 450° for 10-12 minutes or until golden brown. Cool on a wire rack.

● Spread melted chocolate over bottom of crust. Cover and refrigerate for 5-10 minutes or until almost set. Meanwhile, in a large bowl, beat the cream cheese, cream and vanilla until smooth. Gradually beat in the confectioners' sugar. Spread over chocolate layer.

● Arrange strawberries over filling; brush with jelly. Cover and refrigerate for at least 2 hours. Remove sides of pan before serving.

YIELD: 6-8 SERVINGS.

CRUNCHY PEANUT BUTTER TARTS

COOKIE PIZZA A LA MODE

LEMON
BLUEBERRY PIZZA

NO BAKE

PREP/TOTAL TIME: 15 MIN. + COOLING

Cream cheese and lemon yogurt dotted with fresh blueberries make a tasty topping for this delightful fruit pizza.

TASTE OF HOME TEST KITCHEN

1	tube (16-1/2 ounces) refrigerated sugar cookie dough
1	package (8 ounces) cream cheese, softened
2	tablespoons sugar
3/4	cup (6 ounces) lemon yogurt
2	cups fresh blueberries

- Press the cookie dough onto an ungreased 12-in. pizza pan. Bake at 350° for 15-20 minutes or until deep golden brown. Cool on a wire rack.

- In a small bowl, beat the cream cheese and sugar until smooth; stir in the yogurt. Spread over the crust to within 1/2 in. of edges. Sprinkle with blueberries. Cut into wedges. Refrigerate leftovers.

YIELD: 8 SERVINGS.

COOKIE PIZZA
A LA MODE

NO BAKE

PREP/TOTAL TIME: 20 MIN.

This yummy sensation can't be beat—especially because it's so easy to make. It's like eating a chewy chocolate chip cookie and frosty ice cream sundae all in one!

DEE DREW • ALISO VIEJO, CALIFORNIA

1	tube (16-1/2 ounces) refrigerated chocolate chip cookie dough

Chocolate syrup
Vanilla ice cream

6	maraschino cherries, optional

- Press the cookie dough onto an ungreased 12-in. pizza pan. Bake dough at 350° for 15-20 minutes or until deep golden brown. Cool on a wire rack for 5 minutes. Cut into six wedges.

- Drizzle the chocolate syrup over dessert plates. Top with the warm cookie wedges, ice cream and additional chocolate syrup. Garnish with a cherry if desired.

YIELD: 6 SERVINGS.

buying blueberries

When purchasing blueberries, look for those that are firm, dry, plump and smooth-skinned and relatively free from leaves and stems. Berries should be deep purple-blue to blue-black.

LEMON BLUEBERRY PIZZA

CRANBERRY APPLE TART

PREP: 30 MIN. + RISING **BAKE:** 15 MIN. + CHILLING

This light and luscious fruit tart is sweetened with sugar substitute so it's a great treat for those who are diabetic or watching their calories.

TASTE OF HOME TEST KITCHEN

SWEET POTATO TART

- 1/2 teaspoon active dry yeast
- 1 tablespoon warm water (110° to 115°)
- 2 tablespoons beaten egg
- 2 tablespoons butter, softened
- 4-1/2 teaspoons sugar
- 1 teaspoon grated orange peel
- 3/4 cup plus 2 tablespoons all-purpose flour
- 1/4 teaspoon salt

FILLING:
- 1 package (12 ounces) fresh or frozen cranberries
- 1-1/2 cups chopped dried apples
- 1-1/2 cups unsweetened apple juice
- 1-1/4 cups sugar
- Sugar substitute equivalent to 1 cup sugar
- 1/2 cup water
- 1/4 teaspoon salt
- 1/4 cup cornstarch
- 1/3 cup cold water

● In a small bowl, dissolve yeast in warm water. Beat in the egg, butter, sugar and orange peel. Combine flour and salt; beat into yeast mixture on low speed just until mixture holds together.

● Shape into a ball. Place in a small bowl coated with cooking spray, turning once to coat top. Cover and let rise in a warm place for 1-1/4 hours (dough will not double, but will leave a slight indentation when pressed).

● Coat an 11-in. fluted tart pan with removable bottom with cooking spray; set aside. Place dough on a piece of waxed paper. Lightly flour dough and roll into a 13-in. circle. Invert into prepared pan; gently peel off waxed paper.

● Line unpricked tart shell with a double thickness of heavy-duty foil. Bake at 375° for 8 minutes. Remove foil; bake 6 minutes longer or until golden brown. Cool on a wire rack.

● In a large saucepan, combine the first seven filling ingredients. Cook and stir until the mixture comes to a boil and cranberries pop. Combine the cornstarch and cold water until smooth; gradually stir into cranberry mixture. Cook 2 minutes longer or until thickened. Cool for 20 minutes. Pour into the crust. Refrigerate for at least 3 hours before cutting.

YIELD: 14 SERVINGS.

EDITOR'S NOTE: This recipe was tested with Splenda no-calorie sweetener.

crackin' cranberries

With their gorgeous ruby-red color, cranberries are the perfect fruit to use in cooking and baking. When cooking them to make a sauce, cook them until they crack and pop. This allows the sugar to penetrate the tart fruit.

SWEET POTATO TART

PREP: 20 MIN. **BAKE:** 30 MIN. + COOLING

I often reduce the fat in desserts so our family can enjoy them more often. You'd never guess this trimmed-down tart, with its homemade pecan crust and creamy filling, is light.

KATE GAUDRY ● LA JOLLA, CALIFORNIA

- 1-1/2 cups all-purpose flour
- 1/2 cup packed brown sugar
- 1/4 cup cold butter, cubed
- 2 tablespoons chopped pecans, toasted
- 1 egg

CRANBERRY APPLE TART

CARAMEL PEANUT FANTASY

FILLING:

    1   can (15-3/4 ounces) sweet potatoes
   1/2 cup packed brown sugar
   1/2 cup fat-free milk
    2   egg whites
   1/3 cup reduced-fat plain yogurt
    1   tablespoon all-purpose flour
   1/2 teaspoon ground cinnamon
   1/4 teaspoon ground ginger
   1/4 teaspoon ground nutmeg
   1/8 teaspoon ground cloves
Reduced-fat whipped topping, optional

- In a food processor, combine flour, brown sugar, butter and pecans. Cover and pulse until blended. Add egg, pulsing until mixture forms a soft dough. Press onto the bottom and up the sides of a 9-in. fluted tart pan with removable bottom.

- Place pan on a baking sheet. Bake at 400° for 8-10 minutes or until lightly browned. Cool on a wire rack. Reduce heat to 350°.

- Drain the sweet potatoes, reserving 1/4 cup liquid. Place potatoes in a food processor; cover and process until pureed. Add the brown sugar, milk, egg whites, yogurt, flour, cinnamon, ginger, nutmeg, cloves and reserved liquid; cover and process until blended.

- Pour into the crust. Bake for 30-35 minutes or until a knife inserted near the center comes out clean. Cool on a wire rack. Store in the refrigerator. Garnish with the whipped topping if desired.

YIELD: 12 SERVINGS.

CARAMEL PEANUT FANTASY
PREP/TOTAL TIME: 30 MIN. + CHILLING

NO BAKE

Packed with peanuts and gooey with caramel, this do-ahead treat is one sweet dream of a dessert to serve company. It goes together quickly...and will disappear just as fast!

TASTE OF HOME TEST KITCHEN

    2   cups crushed vanilla wafers (about 60 wafers)
   1/3 cup butter, melted
   20   caramels
   15   miniature Snickers candy bars
   1/2 cup caramel ice cream topping
   1/2 cup heavy whipping cream, divided
    2   cups salted peanuts, chopped
   3/4 cup semisweet chocolate chips

- In a small bowl, combine wafer crumbs and butter. Press onto the bottom of a greased 9-in. springform pan. Place on a baking sheet. Bake at 350° for 8-10 minutes. Cool on a wire rack.

- In a heavy saucepan, combine the caramels, candy bars, caramel topping and 1/4 cup cream; cook and stir over low heat until smooth and blended. Remove from the heat; stir in peanuts. Spread over crust. Cover and refrigerate for 1 hour.

- In a saucepan or microwave, melt chocolate chips and remaining cream. Spread over caramel layer. Cover and refrigerate for 1 hour or until serving. Refrigerate leftovers.

YIELD: 12 SERVINGS.

BOURBON PUMPKIN TART WITH WALNUT STREUSEL

BOURBON PUMPKIN TART WITH WALNUT STREUSEL

PREP: 45 MIN. + CHILLING BAKE: 45 MIN.

My husband loves pumpkin pie, so I looked high and low for that "perfect" recipe. But as soon as he tasted this tart, he told me to stop searching, declaring this the best he's ever tried!

BRENDA RYAN • MARSHALL, MISSOURI

2	cups all-purpose flour
1/3	cup sugar
1	teaspoon grated orange peel
1/2	teaspoon salt
2/3	cup cold butter, cubed
1	egg, lightly beaten
1/4	cup heavy whipping cream

FILLING:

1	can (15 ounces) solid-pack pumpkin
3	eggs
1/2	cup sugar
1/2	cup heavy whipping cream
1/4	cup packed brown sugar
1/4	cup bourbon
2	tablespoons all-purpose flour
1	teaspoon ground cinnamon
1	teaspoon ground ginger
1/4	teaspoon salt
1/4	teaspoon ground cloves

TOPPING:

3/4	cup all-purpose flour
1/3	cup sugar
1/3	cup packed brown sugar
1/2	teaspoon salt
1/2	teaspoon ground cinnamon
1/2	cup cold butter, cubed
3/4	cup coarsely chopped walnuts, toasted
1/4	cup chopped crystallized ginger

- In a large bowl, combine the flour, sugar, orange peel and salt. Cut in butter until crumbly. Add egg. Gradually add cream, tossing with a fork until a ball forms. Cover and refrigerate for at least 30 minutes or until easy to handle.

- On a lightly floured surface, roll out pastry into a 13-in. circle. Press onto the bottom and up the sides of an ungreased 11-in. fluted tart pan with removable bottom.

- In a large bowl, combine the filling ingredients. Pour into crust. For topping, combine the flour, sugar, brown sugar, salt and cinnamon. Cut in butter until crumbly. Stir in walnuts and ginger. Sprinkle over filling.

- Bake at 350° for 45-55 minutes or until a knife inserted near the center comes out clean. Cool on a wire rack. Refrigerate leftovers.

YIELD: 14 SERVINGS.

LEMON STRAWBERRY TARTS

PREP/TOTAL TIME: 20 MIN. + CHILLING

Sugar cookies made from convenient refrigerated dough serve as the easy base for these lovely tarts topped with cool lemon curd and fresh fruit.

TASTE OF HOME TEST KITCHEN

1	package (18 ounces) refrigerated sugar cookie dough
3/4	cup chilled lemon curd
6	large fresh strawberries, sliced

Whipped cream

- Cut cookie dough into 1/2-in. slices. Place 2 in. apart on ungreased baking sheets. Bake at 350° for 11-12 minutes or until lightly browned. Remove to wire racks to cool.

- Spread six cookies with 2 tablespoons lemon curd. Garnish with strawberries and whipped cream. Save remaining cookies for another use.

YIELD: 6 TARTS.

LEMON STRAWBERRY TARTS

FRESH FRUIT TARTLETS

FRESH FRUIT TARTLETS (NO BAKE)
PREP/TOTAL TIME: 20 MIN.

These mini tarts are perfect for showers, parties or whenever you need a pretty dessert. Top them with berries, bananas, mandarin oranges or the fruit of your choice.

SHELLY FORSLUND • NASHOTAH, WISCONSIN

1	envelope whipped topping mix (Dream Whip)
1/2	cup cold milk
1	teaspoon vanilla extract
1	package (8 ounces) cream cheese, softened
1/2	cup confectioners' sugar
10	individual graham cracker tart shells

Assorted fresh fruit

- In a small bowl, beat the topping mix, milk and vanilla on low speed until blended. Beat on high until soft peaks form, about 4 minutes. In a large bowl, beat cream cheese and confectioners' sugar until smooth. Fold in whipped topping mixture.

- Spoon into tart shells; top with fruit. Refrigerate leftovers.

YIELD: 10 SERVINGS.

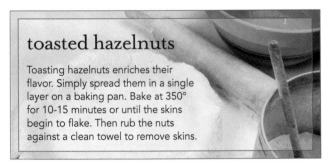

toasted hazelnuts

Toasting hazelnuts enriches their flavor. Simply spread them in a single layer on a baking pan. Bake at 350° for 10-15 minutes or until the skins begin to flake. Then rub the nuts against a clean towel to remove skins.

CHOCOLATE HAZELNUT TART
PREP: 30 MIN. + CHILLING BAKE: 25 MIN. + COOLING

This dessert looks impressive but is actually quite easy to make. I like to serve it with vanilla or coffee ice cream.

GILDA LESTER • MILLSBORO, DELAWARE

6	tablespoons butter, softened
2	tablespoons cream cheese, softened
1/3	cup confectioners' sugar
1	teaspoon grated lemon peel
1	cup all-purpose flour

FILLING:

4	eggs
3/4	cup sugar
1/2	cup chocolate syrup
1/4	cup dark corn syrup
1	cup chopped hazelnuts, toasted
1	cup (6 ounces) miniature semisweet chocolate chips

Whipped cream and chocolate shavings, optional

- In a small bowl, beat butter, cream cheese, confectioners' sugar and lemon peel until creamy. Beat in the flour just until combined.

- Shape the dough into a disk. Wrap in plastic wrap and refrigerate for 30 minutes or until easy to handle.

- Roll dough into an 11-in. circle. Press onto bottom and up the sides of an ungreased 9-in. fluted tart pan with a removable bottom. Bake at 350° for 18-22 minutes or until lightly browned. Cool on a wire rack.

- In a small bowl, combine the eggs, sugar, chocolate syrup and corn syrup. Pour into crust. Combine hazelnuts and chocolate chips; sprinkle over filling. Place pan on a baking sheet.

- Bake for 25-30 minutes or until center is almost set (center will set when cool). Cool on a wire rack.

- Garnish with whipped cream and chocolate shavings if desired. Refrigerate leftovers.

YIELD: 12 SERVINGS.

CHOCOLATE HAZELNUT TART

COBBLERS, CRUMBLES & MORE

LOOK HERE FOR A HOST OF TREATS CALLING

FOR YOUR FAVORITE BAKING INGREDIENTS.

THESE LUSCIOUS DESSERTS MAKE IT EASY AS PIE

TO END DINNER ON A SWEET NOTE.

BLUEBERRY COBBLER

CHERRY PEACH COBBLER

CHERRY PEACH COBBLER
PREP: 15 MIN. BAKE: 20 MIN.

There's no pitting cherries and peeling peaches when you're throwing together this quick cobbler. It calls for convenient canned fruit and purchased pie filling.

SANDRA PIERCE • NORTH BONNEVILLE, WASHINGTON

- 1 can (21 ounces) cherry pie filling
- 1 can (8-1/2 ounces) sliced peaches, drained and halved
- 2 teaspoons lemon juice
- 1/2 teaspoon ground cinnamon

BISCUIT TOPPING:
- 1 cup biscuit/baking mix
- 4 teaspoons sugar, divided
- 3 tablespoons milk
- 2 tablespoons butter, melted
- 1 teaspoon grated lemon peel
- 1/8 teaspoon ground cinnamon
- 3 cups vanilla ice cream

- In a greased microwave-safe 8-in. square baking dish, combine pie filling, peaches, lemon juice and cinnamon. Microwave, uncovered, on high for 3-4 minutes or until heated through, stirring once.

- In a small bowl, combine the biscuit mix, 3 teaspoons sugar, milk, butter and lemon peel. Drop by rounded tablespoonfuls onto filling. Combine the cinnamon and remaining sugar; sprinkle over topping.

- Bake at 400° for 17-19 minutes or until golden brown. Serve warm with ice cream.

YIELD: 6 SERVINGS.

EDITOR'S NOTE: This recipe was tested in a 1,100-watt microwave.

MINI APPLE PIES
PREP/TOTAL TIME: 30 MIN.

My kids set up an assembly line when making these snacks—one chops the apples and mixes the filling, one rolls out the biscuits and one puts the pies together.

MARSHA DINGBAUM • AURORA, CALIFORNIA

- 1 tube (12 ounces) refrigerated buttermilk biscuits
- 1 medium tart apple, peeled and finely chopped
- 1/4 cup raisins
- 3 tablespoons sugar
- 1 teaspoon ground cinnamon
- 2 tablespoons butter

- Using a rolling pin, flatten each biscuit into a 3-in. to 4-in. circle. Combine the apple, raisins, sugar and cinnamon; place a tablespoonful on each biscuit. Dot with the butter. Bring up sides of biscuit to enclose filling and pinch to seal.

- Place in ungreased muffin cups. Bake at 375° for 11-13 minutes or until golden brown.

YIELD: 10 SERVINGS.

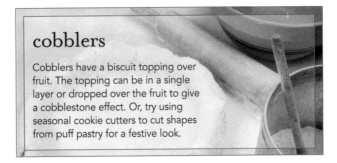

cobblers

Cobblers have a biscuit topping over fruit. The topping can be in a single layer or dropped over the fruit to give a cobblestone effect. Or, try using seasonal cookie cutters to cut shapes from puff pastry for a festive look.

MINI APPLE PIES

PEAR PANDOWDY

PREP: 20 MIN. BAKE: 20 MIN.

I pulled out this recipe one night when my husband was craving something sweet, and it was a big hit with both of us. It's a great last-minute dessert that melts in your mouth.

JENNIFER CLASS • SNOHOMISH, WASHINGTON

- 2 medium firm pears, peeled and sliced
- 2 tablespoons brown sugar
- 4-1/2 teaspoons butter
- 1-1/2 teaspoons lemon juice
- 1/8 teaspoon ground cinnamon
- 1/8 teaspoon ground nutmeg

TOPPING:
- 1/2 cup all-purpose flour
- 2 tablespoons plus 1/2 teaspoon sugar, divided
- 1/2 teaspoon baking powder
- 1/8 teaspoon salt
- 1/4 cup cold butter, cubed
- 2 tablespoons water

Vanilla ice cream, optional

- In a small saucepan, combine the first six ingredients. Cook and stir over medium heat for 5 minutes or until pears are tender. Pour into a greased 3-cup baking dish.

- In a small bowl, combine the flour, 2 tablespoons sugar, baking powder and salt; cut in butter until crumbly. Stir in water. Sprinkle over the pear mixture. Sprinkle with the remaining sugar.

- Bake, uncovered, at 375° for 20-25 minutes or until a toothpick inserted into topping comes out clean and topping is lightly browned. Serve warm with ice cream if desired.

YIELD: 2 SERVINGS.

PEAR PANDOWDY

BLUEBERRY BUCKLE

PREP: 20 MIN. BAKE: 45 MIN.

I love baking and wanted to try my hand at an old-fashioned recipe. A buckle is a cake-like dessert made with berries and may or may not have a crumb topping. It got its name because the cake sometimes buckles under the weight of the topping.

JO-ANNE STACEY • KELLIGREWS, NEWFOUNDLAND AND LABRADOR

- 1/4 cup shortening
- 1/2 cup sugar
- 1 egg
- 1 cup all-purpose flour
- 1-1/2 teaspoons baking powder
- 1/2 teaspoon salt
- 1/2 cup milk
- 2 cups fresh or frozen blueberries

TOPPING:
- 1/4 cup butter
- 1/2 cup sugar
- 1/3 cup all-purpose flour
- 1/2 teaspoon ground cinnamon

- In a medium bowl, cream shortening and sugar. Beat in egg. Combine the flour, baking powder and salt; add alternately with milk to creamed mixture. Pour into an ungreased 8-in. square baking pan. Arrange blueberries on top.

- In another bowl, cream butter and sugar. Combine flour and cinnamon; add gradually to the creamed mixture. Crumble over blueberries. Bake at 350° for 45-50 minutes.

YIELD: 8 SERVINGS.

CHOCOLATE CHERRY DESSERT

PREP/TOTAL TIME: 30 MIN.

Chocolate and cherries are the perfect partners in this lip-smacking delight. Guests will be asking you for the recipe!

CHERRY TURNER • EUNICE, LOUISIANA

- 26 chocolate wafer cookies, crushed
- 1/4 cup butter, melted
- 1 cup (8 ounces) sour cream
- 1 package (3.9 ounces) instant chocolate pudding mix
- 3/4 cup milk
- 1 can (21 ounces) cherry pie filling

- In a bowl, combine wafer crumbs with butter. Press into an 8-in. square dish. Place in freezer for 10 minutes.

- In another bowl, combine sour cream, pudding and milk; beat on low for 1-1/2 minutes. Spread over crust. Spoon pie filling on top. Cover and refrigerate until serving.

YIELD: 9 SERVINGS.

SPICED PEAR CRUMBLE
PREP: 25 MIN. BAKE: 20 MIN.

Guests at my bed-and-breakfast rave about this crumble. They get to enjoy a sweet treat that doesn't expand their waistline.

BARBRA ANNINO • GALENA, ILLINOIS

4	medium pears, peeled and chopped
1/4	cup dried cranberries
2	teaspoons lemon juice
2	tablespoons reduced-fat butter
1/2	cup reduced-sugar orange marmalade
1/4	cup sugar-free maple-flavored syrup
1/2	teaspoon ground cinnamon
1/4	teaspoon ground ginger
1/8	teaspoon ground allspice
1	teaspoon vanilla extract
1-1/2	cups crushed reduced-fat vanilla wafers (about 45 wafers)
1/4	cup chopped almonds
1-1/2	cups reduced-fat vanilla ice cream

- In a small bowl, combine pears, cranberries and lemon juice. Transfer to an 8-in. square baking dish coated with cooking spray; set aside.

- In a small saucepan, melt butter over medium heat. Stir in the marmalade, syrup, cinnamon, ginger and allspice until blended. Bring to a boil. Remove from the heat; stir in vanilla. Drizzle evenly over pear mixture. Sprinkle with vanilla wafers and almonds.

- Bake, uncovered, at 375° for 20-25 minutes or until pears are tender and topping is golden brown. Serve warm with ice cream.

YIELD: 6 SERVINGS.

EDITOR'S NOTE: This recipe was tested with Land O'Lakes light stick butter.

pear pointers

Select firm pears for baking. Use a vegetable peeler or paring knife to remove the skin, which turns dark and tough when exposed to heat. To prevent pear slices from discoloration, simply toss with a little lemon juice.

APPLE PEACH COBBLER

APPLE PEACH COBBLER
PREP: 20 MIN. BAKE: 25 MIN.

Take advantage of good prices on fresh fruit in season for this wonderful cobbler. It's full of old-fashioned goodness.

ANNA MINEGAR • ZOLFO SPRINGS, FLORIDA

    4   cups sliced peeled peaches or frozen
        unsweetened peach slices, thawed
    1   medium tart apple, peeled and thinly sliced
  1/3   cup sugar
  1/3   cup packed brown sugar
    1   teaspoon ground cinnamon
  1/4   teaspoon ground nutmeg
TOPPING:
    1   cup all-purpose flour
    1   tablespoon sugar
    1   teaspoon baking powder
  1/4   teaspoon salt
    2   tablespoons cold butter
  1/2   cup whole milk
1-1/2   cups vanilla ice cream

- In a large bowl, combine the first six ingredients. Spoon into a greased shallow 2-qt. baking dish.

- For topping, in a bowl, combine flour, sugar, baking powder and salt. Cut in butter until crumbly. Stir in milk just until blended. Drop by spoonfuls over peach mixture.

- Bake at 400° for 25-30 minutes or until filling is bubbly and topping is golden brown. Serve warm with ice cream.
YIELD: 6 SERVINGS.

PLUM BUMBLE
PREP: 10 MIN. BAKE: 45 MIN.

I've served this recipe numerous times since it was first published in our local paper in 1976. It is always a favorite at gatherings.

ARLIS ENBURG • ROCK ISLAND, ILLINOIS

    1   cup plus 5 teaspoons sugar, divided
  1/4   cup cornstarch
    3   cups sliced fresh plums (about 1-1/4 pounds)
  3/4   cup pineapple tidbits
    2   tablespoons butter, melted

1/2 teaspoon ground cinnamon
1 tube (7-1/2 ounces) refrigerated buttermilk biscuits, separated and quartered

- In a large bowl, combine 1 cup sugar, cornstarch, plums and pineapple. Transfer to a greased shallow 2-qt. baking dish; dot with 1 tablespoon butter. Bake, uncovered, at 400° for 15 minutes.
- Meanwhile, melt remaining butter. In a small bowl, combine cinnamon and remaining sugar. Place biscuit pieces over hot plum mixture; brush with butter and sprinkle with cinnamon-sugar. Bake 25-30 minutes longer or until biscuits are golden brown.

YIELD: 6 SERVINGS.

BLUEBERRY GRUNT
NO BAKE

PREP: 15 MIN. COOK: 30 MIN.

A tightly covered skillet will "grunt" while this special dessert cooks. I like to make it when fresh blueberries are in season.

IOLA EGLE • BELLA VISTA, ARKANSAS

4 cups fresh blueberries
1 cup sugar
1 cup water
1-1/2 cups all-purpose flour
2 teaspoons baking powder
2 tablespoons grated orange peel
1/2 teaspoon ground cinnamon
1/4 teaspoon ground nutmeg
1/4 teaspoon salt
3/4 cup milk
Heavy whipping cream, optional

- In a skillet, combine the blueberries, sugar and water; bring to a boil. Simmer, uncovered, for 20 minutes.
- In a bowl, combine the next six ingredients; stir in the milk just until moistened (dough will be stiff). Drop by tablespoonfuls over blueberries.
- Cover and cook for 10-15 minutes or until the dumplings are puffed and test done. Serve warm with the heavy whipping cream if desired.

YIELD: 6-8 SERVINGS.

crisps

Crisps have a crumb topping over the fruit. The topping has flour, sugar and butter and may or may not have oats, nuts and spices. The topping gets crisp while baking, hence its name.

CARAMEL APPLE CRISP DESSERT
PREP: 20 MIN. BAKE: 45 MIN.

This traditional New England crisp is one of my most requested recipes. Although it makes a fairly big batch, it doesn't take long for it to get gobbled up.

JANET SICIAK • BERNARDSTON, MASSACHUSETTS

1/2 cup all-purpose flour
1/2 cup sugar
1/2 teaspoon ground cinnamon
1/4 teaspoon ground nutmeg
40 caramels, quartered
9 cups sliced peeled baking apples
1/4 cup orange juice
TOPPING:
1/2 cup sugar
1/3 cup all-purpose flour
3 tablespoons cold butter
2/3 cup quick-cooking oats
1/2 cup chopped walnuts

- In a bowl, combine the flour, sugar, cinnamon and nutmeg; add caramels and stir to coat.
- In another bowl, toss apples with orange juice. Add caramel mixture and mix. Spread into a greased 13-in. x 9-in. baking dish.
- For topping, combine sugar and flour in a small bowl; cut in butter until crumbly. Add oats and walnuts; sprinkle over apples. Bake, uncovered, at 350° for 45-50 minutes or until apples are tender.

YIELD: 16-20 SERVINGS.

CARAMEL APPLE CRISP DESSERT

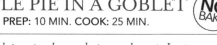

APPLE PIE IN A GOBLET

TRIPLE-BERRY COBBLER
PREP: 20 MIN. BAKE: 25 MIN.

I combined several recipes to come up with this one. It's very versatile. Sometimes I use other fruits depending on what is available or on hand.

EDNA WOODARD • FREDERICKSBURG, TEXAS

1/2	cup sugar
3	tablespoons cornstarch
1/4	teaspoon ground cinnamon
1	cup water
1	cup fresh or frozen cranberries, thawed
1	cup fresh blueberries
1	cup fresh blackberries

TOPPING:

1/4	cup sugar
2	tablespoons butter, softened
1/3	cup fat-free milk
1/4	teaspoon vanilla extract
2/3	cup all-purpose flour
3/4	teaspoon baking powder
1/4	teaspoon salt

- In a small heavy saucepan, combine sugar, cornstarch, cinnamon and water until smooth. Bring to a boil; cook and stir for 2 minutes or until thickened. Remove from the heat; stir in berries. Transfer to an 8-in. square baking dish coated with cooking spray.

- For topping, in a small bowl, beat the sugar and butter until crumbly, about 2 minutes. Beat in milk and vanilla. Combine flour, baking powder and salt; stir into butter mixture just until blended. Drop by tablespoonfuls over fruit mixture.

- Bake at 375° for 25-30 minutes or until filling is bubbly and a toothpick inserted in topping comes out clean. Serve warm.

YIELD: 6 SERVINGS.

APPLE PIE IN A GOBLET
PREP: 10 MIN. COOK: 25 MIN.

NO BAKE

This dish is not only easy but very elegant. I got the recipe from a church cooking class and now fix it often. You can serve it in bowls, but I always get more oohs and aahs when I put it in lovely goblets.

RENEE ZIMMER • GIG HARBOR, WASHINGTON

3	large tart apples, peeled and coarsely chopped
1/4	cup sugar
1/4	cup water
3/4	teaspoon ground cinnamon
1/4	teaspoon ground nutmeg
12	shortbread cookies, crushed
2	cups vanilla ice cream

Whipped cream

- In a large saucepan, combine the apples, sugar, water, cinnamon and nutmeg. Bring to a boil. Reduce the heat; cover and simmer for 10 minutes or until apples are tender. Uncover; cook 9-11 minutes longer or until most of the liquid has evaporated. Remove from heat.

- In each of four goblets or parfait glasses, layer 1 tablespoon cookie crumbs, 1/2 cup ice cream and a fourth of the apple mixture. Top with remaining cookie crumbs and whipped cream. Serve immediately.

YIELD: 4 SERVINGS.

TRIPLE-BERRY COBBLER

APPLE DANISH PIES

APPLE DANISH PIES
PREP: 25 MIN. BAKE: 20 MIN.

Prepared with an easy crescent roll crust and served in cute ramekins, these single-serving pies are fun to share.

JOANNE WRIGHT • NILES, MICHIGAN

1/3	cup sugar
1	tablespoon plus 1 teaspoon cornstarch
1/2	teaspoon ground cinnamon
1/8	teaspoon ground nutmeg
2	cups chopped peeled tart apples
1/4	cup unsweetened apple juice
1	tube (4 ounces) refrigerated crescent rolls
1	package (3 ounces) cream cheese, softened
2	tablespoons confectioners' sugar
1/2	teaspoon vanilla extract

GLAZE:

1/4	cup confectioners' sugar
2	teaspoons 2% milk

- In a small saucepan, combine sugar, cornstarch, cinnamon and nutmeg. Add apples and juice; toss to coat. Bring to a boil; cook and stir for 2 minutes or until thickened. Remove from the heat.

- Separate the crescent dough into four triangles. On a lightly floured surface, roll two triangles into 5-in. circles. Place each triangle into an 8-oz. ramekin, pressing the dough onto the bottom and 1/2 in. up the sides.

- In a small bowl, beat the cream cheese, confectioners' sugar and vanilla. Spread over the dough in the ramekins. Top with apple mixture. Roll out the remaining crescent dough triangles into two 4-in. circles; place over filling. Cut slits in top.

- Bake at 375° for 20-25 minutes or until the filling is bubbly and the topping is golden brown. Combine the confectioners' sugar and milk; drizzle over pies. Serve warm.

YIELD: 2 SERVINGS.

PLUM CRISP

PLUM CRISP
PREP: 15 MIN. BAKE: 50 MIN.

*We just love plums, so I developed this new twist on
the traditional apple crisp to satisfy our cravings. This tart
and sweet treat bakes up golden brown and crunchy.*

OLIVIA SMITH • RICHMOND, MASSACHUSETTS

3	medium plums, sliced

Dash ground nutmeg

1/4	cup all-purpose flour
1/4	cup sugar
1/4	cup old-fashioned oats
3	tablespoons butter, melted
1/4	teaspoon almond extract

- Arrange plums in a 7-in. pie plate coated with cooking spray. Sprinkle with nutmeg; set aside. In a small bowl, combine the flour, sugar and oats; stir in butter and extract. Sprinkle over plums.

- Cover and bake at 350° for 40 minutes; uncover and bake 10-15 minutes longer or until filling is bubbly and topping is golden brown. Serve warm.

YIELD: 3 SERVINGS.

APRICOT COBBLER
PREP: 15 MIN. BAKE: 55 MIN.

*Even folks who watch their diets deserve to splurge on dessert.
This light cobbler, featuring apricots, is simply delicious.*

MRS. CURTIS JEFFERY • BURR OAK, KANSAS

1	can (29 ounces) light apricot halves
1	package (.8 ounce) sugar-free cook-and-serve vanilla pudding mix
1	cup all-purpose flour
1/4	teaspoon salt
1/3	cup cold butter, cubed
1/4	cup water

- Drain apricots, reserving juice. In a bowl, whisk the juice and pudding mix until smooth; stir in apricots. Pour into an 8-in. square baking dish coated with cooking spray; set aside.

- In a bowl, combine the flour and salt; cut in butter until crumbly. Gradually add water, tossing with fork until dough forms a ball. On a floured surface, roll out dough to fit top of baking dish; place over filling. Trim and flute edges; cut slits in top.

- Bake at 450° for 15 minutes. Reduce heat to 350°; bake 40-45 minutes longer or until crust is golden brown and filling is bubbly.

YIELD: 9 SERVINGS.

LITTLE LEMON MERINGUE PIES

PREP: 25 MIN. + CHILLING BAKE: 25 MIN. + COOLING

My husband and I love these cute mini lemon pies. The recipe is supposed to serve two, but they're so scrumptious, they sometimes only serve one!

KATHY ZIELICKE • FOND DU LAC, WISCONSIN

1/3	cup all-purpose flour
1/8	teaspoon salt
1	tablespoon shortening
1	tablespoon cold butter
1	teaspoon cold water

FILLING:

1/3	cup sugar
1	tablespoon cornstarch
1/8	teaspoon salt
1/2	cup cold water
1	egg yolk, beaten
2	tablespoons lemon juice
1	tablespoon butter

MERINGUE:

1	egg white
1/8	teaspoon cream of tartar
2	tablespoons sugar

- In a bowl, combine flour and salt; cut in shortening and butter until crumbly. Gradually add the water, tossing with a fork until dough forms a ball. Divide in half. Roll each portion into a 5-in. circle. Transfer to two 10-oz. custard cups. Press dough 1-1/8 in. up sides of cups. Place on a baking sheet. Bake at 425° for 7-10 minutes or until golden brown.

- In a saucepan, combine the sugar, cornstarch and salt. Gradually stir in the cold water until smooth. Cook and stir over medium heat until thickened and bubbly. Reduce heat; cook and stir 2 minutes more. Remove from the heat.

- Stir half of hot filling into egg yolk; return all to the pan. Bring to a gentle boil; cook and stir for 2 minutes. Remove from the heat; stir in lemon juice and butter.

- Pour into pastry shells. In a small bowl, beat the egg white and cream of tartar on medium speed until soft peaks form. Spread evenly over the hot filling, sealing edges to crust. Bake at 350° for 15-20 minutes or until meringue is golden brown. Cool on a wire rack for 1 hour; refrigerate for at least 3 hours before serving.

YIELD: 2 SERVINGS.

LIME 'N' SPICE PEACH COBBLER

PREP: 25 MIN. BAKE: 35 MIN.

This was my grandmother's favorite recipe to make when peaches were in season. Now I bake it all the time for my family and friends.

MARY ANN DELL • PHOENIXVILLE, PENNSYLVANIA

8	medium peaches, peeled and sliced
3	tablespoons sugar
3	tablespoons brown sugar
2	tablespoons minced crystallized ginger
4-1/2	teaspoons cornstarch
1	tablespoon lime juice
2	teaspoons ground cinnamon
1/2	teaspoon grated lime peel

TOPPING:

1/4	cup packed brown sugar
2	tablespoons sugar
3	tablespoons butter, softened
1	cup cake flour
1/2	teaspoon baking powder
1/4	teaspoon salt
2	tablespoons cold water
1/4	cup chopped pecans
2	tablespoons buttermilk
1	egg yolk

- In a large bowl, combine first eight ingredients. Transfer to an 8-in. square baking dish coated with cooking spray.

- For topping, in a small bowl, beat the sugars and butter until crumbly, about 2 minutes. Combine the flour, baking powder and salt and gradually add to the butter mixture. Beat in the water just until moistened (mixture will be crumbly). Stir in the pecans. Crumble over the fruit mixture.

- Combine buttermilk and egg yolk; drizzle over topping. Bake at 375° for 35-40 minutes or until filling is bubbly and topping is golden brown. Serve warm.

YIELD: 8 SERVINGS.

LIME 'N' SPICE PEACH COBBLER

PEACH CRUMBLE DESSERT

PEACH CRUMBLE DESSERT
PREP: 15 MIN. BAKE: 35 MIN.

*This easy-to-make crumble is delicious and has
old-fashioned appeal. It's delectable served with ice cream.*

NANCY HORSBURGH • EVERETT, ONTARIO

6	cups sliced peeled ripe peaches
1/4	cup packed brown sugar
3	tablespoons all-purpose flour
1	teaspoon lemon juice
1/2	teaspoon grated lemon peel
1/2	teaspoon ground cinnamon

TOPPING:

1	cup all-purpose flour
1	cup sugar
1	teaspoon baking powder
1/4	teaspoon salt
1/4	teaspoon ground nutmeg
1	egg, lightly beaten
1/2	cup butter, melted and cooled

Vanilla ice cream, optional

- Place peaches in a greased shallow 2-1/2-qt. baking dish. In a small bowl, combine the brown sugar, flour, lemon juice, lemon peel and cinnamon; sprinkle over the peaches.

- Combine the flour, sugar, baking powder, salt and nutmeg. Stir in egg until the mixture resembles coarse crumbs. Sprinkle over the peaches. Pour butter evenly over topping.

- Bake at 375° for 35-40 minutes. Serve with ice cream if desired.

YIELD: 10-12 SERVINGS.

CARAMEL APPLE CRISP
PREP: 20 MIN. BAKE: 45 MIN.

Use a variety of apples in this crisp for a nice flavor combination.

MICHELLE BROOKS • CLARKSTON, MICHIGAN

3	cups old-fashioned oats
2	cups all-purpose flour
1-1/2	cups packed brown sugar
1	teaspoon ground cinnamon
1	cup cold butter
8	cups thinly sliced peeled tart apples
1	package (14 ounces) caramels, halved
1	cup apple cider, divided

- In a large bowl, combine the oats, flour, brown sugar and cinnamon; cut in the butter until crumbly. Press half of the mixture into a greased 13-in. x 9-in. baking dish. Layer with half of the apples, caramels and 1 cup oat mixture. Repeat the layers. Pour 1/2 cup of cider over the top.

- Bake, uncovered, at 350° for 30 minutes. Drizzle with the remaining cider; bake 15-20 minutes longer or until apples are tender.

YIELD: 12-14 SERVINGS.

BLUEBERRY COBBLER
PREP: 20 MIN. BAKE: 30 MIN.

*With a crisp biscuit topping and warm blueberry filling,
this home-style cobbler is guaranteed to please!*

MARY RELYEA • CANASTOTA, NEW YORK

4	cups fresh or frozen blueberries, thawed
3/4	cup sugar, divided
3	tablespoons cornstarch
2	tablespoons lemon juice
1/4	teaspoon ground cinnamon
1/8	teaspoon ground nutmeg
1	cup all-purpose flour
2	teaspoons grated lemon peel
3/4	teaspoon baking powder
1/4	teaspoon salt
1/4	teaspoon baking soda
3	tablespoons cold butter
3/4	cup buttermilk

- In a large bowl, combine the blueberries, 1/2 cup sugar, cornstarch, lemon juice, cinnamon and nutmeg. Transfer to a 2-qt. baking dish coated with cooking spray.

- In a small bowl, combine the flour, lemon peel, baking powder, salt, baking soda and remaining sugar; cut in butter until crumbly. Stir in buttermilk just until moistened. Drop by tablespoonfuls onto blueberry mixture.

- Bake, uncovered, at 375° for 30-35 minutes. Serve warm.

YIELD: 8 SERVINGS.

BLUEBERRY COBBLER

TROPICAL CRISP
PREP: 20 MIN. **BAKE:** 30 MIN.

One bite of this sweet, juicy, crunchy crisp, and you'll swear you hear the crash of the ocean and feel warm sand under your toes!

TASTE OF HOME TEST KITCHEN

1	fresh pineapple, peeled and cubed
4	medium bananas, sliced
1/4	cup packed brown sugar
2	tablespoons all-purpose flour

TOPPING:

1/3	cup old-fashioned oats
1/4	cup all-purpose flour
2	tablespoons flaked coconut, toasted
2	tablespoons brown sugar
1/4	teaspoon ground nutmeg
1/4	cup cold butter, cubed

- In a large bowl, combine the pineapple and bananas. Sprinkle with brown sugar and flour; toss to coat.

Transfer mixture to an 11-in. x 7-in. baking dish coated with cooking spray.

- In a small bowl, combine the oats, flour, coconut, brown sugar and nutmeg. Cut in butter until crumbly. Sprinkle over pineapple mixture.

- Bake at 350° for 30-35 minutes or until filling is bubbly and topping is golden brown. Serve warm or at room temperature.

YIELD: 9 SERVINGS.

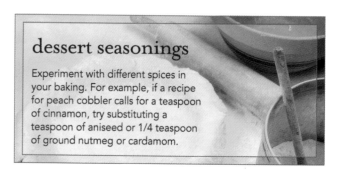

dessert seasonings

Experiment with different spices in your baking. For example, if a recipe for peach cobbler calls for a teaspoon of cinnamon, try substituting a teaspoon of aniseed or 1/4 teaspoon of ground nutmeg or cardamom.

FRUIT KUCHEN
PREP: 15 MIN. **BAKE:** 25 MIN.

You'll find this recipe quicker and easier than traditional fruit kuchen because it calls for frozen bread dough versus handmade.

SANDRA FISCHER • STURGIS, SOUTH DAKOTA

- 1 cup heavy whipping cream
- 3/4 cup sugar
- 2/3 cup soft bread crumbs
- 1 loaf (1 pound) frozen bread dough, thawed
- 3 tablespoons cherry or raspberry pie filling

TOPPING:
- 3 tablespoons all-purpose flour
- 2 tablespoons butter, melted
- 1 tablespoon sugar

- In a saucepan, combine the cream, sugar and bread crumbs. Cook over medium heat until mixture begins to thicken. Remove from the heat; cook for 15 minutes.

- Meanwhile, divide the dough in half; press onto the bottom and up the sides of two 9-in. pie plates to form a crust.

- Pour half of the cream mixture into each crust. Drop spoonfuls of pie filling over cream layer. Combine the topping ingredients; sprinkle over filling.

- Bake at 350° for 25-30 minutes or until the edges are golden brown and center is set.

YIELD: 2 KUCHENS (8-10 SERVINGS EACH).

CHERRY GRUNT
PREP: 15 MIN. **COOK:** 30 MIN.

Give this old-fashioned dessert a try the next time you have a hankering for the flavor of cherry pie.

JUDY MEIKLE • CHEROKEE, IOWA

- 1 can (16 ounces) pitted tart red cherries, undrained
- 1-1/2 cups water
- 3/4 cup sugar, divided
- 1/4 cup butter, divided
- 1 cup all-purpose flour
- 1-1/2 teaspoons baking powder

Pinch salt
- 1/3 cup milk
- 1/2 teaspoon vanilla extract

- Place cherries and juice in a large saucepan or Dutch oven along with water, 1/2 cup sugar and 2 tablespoons butter. Simmer for 5 minutes.

- Meanwhile, sift together flour, baking powder, salt and remaining sugar; place in a bowl. Cut in the remaining butter with a pastry blender. Add milk and vanilla.

- Drop by teaspoonfuls over cherry mixture; cover and simmer for 20 minutes.

YIELD: 8-10 SERVINGS.

DEEP-FRIED CHERRY PIES
PREP/TOTAL TIME: 30 MIN.

With a wonderfully flaky crust, these stuffed cherry pies always make a quick treat. My family loves them for dessert, but they're also great for a snack-on-the-go.

MONICA LARKIN • SHINNSTON, WEST VIRGINIA

- 1 cup all-purpose flour
- 1/4 teaspoon baking powder
- 1/4 teaspoon salt
- 2 tablespoons shortening
- 1/3 cup boiling water
- 1 cup cherry pie filling

Oil for deep-fat frying
- 1/4 cup maple syrup
- 1/4 cup whipped topping

- In a small bowl, combine the flour, baking powder and salt. Cut in shortening until mixture resembles coarse crumbs. Stir in water just until moistened. Turn onto a lightly floured surface; knead 8-10 times.

- Divide dough into four portions; roll each into an 8-in. circle. Place 1/4 cup of pie filling in the center of each circle. Fold dough over filling; secure with toothpicks.

- In an electric skillet, heat 1 in. of oil to 375°. Fry pies, folded side down, in oil for 2-3 minutes or until lightly browned. Turn and fry 2-3 minutes longer. Drain on paper towels. Remove toothpicks. Serve with syrup and whipped topping.

YIELD: 4 SERVINGS.

DEEP-FRIED CHERRY PIES

PRETZEL FRUIT PIZZA

PRETZEL FRUIT PIZZA
PREP: 50 MIN. + CHILLING

I created this recipe while working as an independent kitchen consultant for a national company. It's wonderful!

BETHANY PERRY • BEVERLY, MASSACHUSETTS

    3 cups finely crushed pretzels
  2/3 cup sugar
1-1/4 cups cold butter
    1 can (14 ounces) sweetened condensed milk
  1/4 cup lime juice
    1 tablespoon grated lime peel
1-1/2 cups whipped topping
    7 to 8 cups assorted fresh fruit

- In a large bowl, combine the pretzels and sugar. Cut in the butter until mixture resembles coarse crumbs. Press into a 14-in. pizza pan.

- Bake at 375° for 8-10 minutes or until set. Cool on a wire rack; refrigerate for 30 minutes.

- Meanwhile, in a bowl, combine the milk, lime juice and peel. Fold in whipped topping; spread over crust. Cover and chill. Top with fruit just before serving.

YIELD: 8 SERVINGS.

APPLE BROWN BETTY
PREP: 15 MIN. **BAKE:** 55 MIN.

A light spin on a down-home traditional treat, this recipe has all of the comforting taste of the original.

DALE HARTMAN • COVENTRY, RHODE ISLAND

    6 cups sliced peeled Golden Delicious apples
Sugar substitute equivalent to 1/3 cup sugar
  1/4 teaspoon ground cinnamon
    2 slices reduced-calorie whole wheat bread
    2 tablespoons reduced-fat butter, melted
  1/2 cup orange juice

  1/3 cup fat-free whipped cream cheese
  1/2 cup reduced-fat whipped topping

- Place apple slices in a bowl. Combine sugar substitute and cinnamon; sprinkle over the apples and toss to coat evenly. Place the bread in a food processor; cover and process until fine crumbs form. In a small bowl, combine bread crumbs and butter until blended.

- Place half of apple mixture in an 8-in. square baking dish coated with cooking spray. Top with about 1/3 cup crumb mixture and remaining apple mixture. Pour orange juice over apples. Cover and bake at 350° for 30 minutes. Uncover; sprinkle with remaining crumb mixture. Bake 25-30 minutes longer or until apples are tender and crumb topping is golden brown.

- In a bowl, beat cream cheese until smooth. Beat in half of the whipped topping. Fold in the remaining whipped topping. Serve with Apple Brown Betty.

YIELD: 6 SERVINGS.

EDITOR'S NOTE: This recipe was tested with Splenda No Calorie Sweetener and Land O'Lakes light stick butter. Look for Splenda in the baking aisle of your grocery store.

TORTILLA FRUIT PIE
PREP/TOTAL TIME: 30 MIN.

Here's a fun, no-fuss way to fix dessert for one. Simply cook fresh peach slices with lemon juice, brown sugar and almond extract and bake inside a folded flour tortilla. It's sure to sweeten any meal.

ANN SOBOTKA • GLENDALE, ARIZONA

    3 teaspoons butter, divided
    1 tablespoon brown sugar
    2 teaspoons lemon juice
  1/8 teaspoon almond extract
    1 large ripe peach, peeled and sliced
    1 flour tortilla (10 inches)
    1 teaspoon sugar

TORTILLA FRUIT PIE

RHUBARB MALLOW COBBLER

- In a small saucepan, melt 2 teaspoons butter. Stir in the brown sugar, lemon juice and extract. Add peach slices. Cook and stir over medium-low heat for 5 minutes.

- Place tortilla on an ungreased baking sheet. Spoon peach mixture onto half of tortilla to within 1/2 in. of sides; fold tortilla over. Melt remaining butter; brush over the top. Sprinkle with sugar. Bake at 350° for 15-20 minutes or until golden brown. Cut in half.

YIELD: 1 SERVING.

RHUBARB MALLOW COBBLER
PREP: 15 MIN. BAKE: 50 MIN.

My mom used to make this every year when I was growing up. Now we take fresh rhubarb to my son in Texas so he can share this dessert with his family.

JUDY KAY WARWICK • WEBSTER CITY, IOWA

4	cups diced fresh or frozen rhubarb
2-1/2	cups sugar, divided
1	cup miniature marshmallows
1/2	cup butter, softened
1	teaspoon vanilla extract
1-3/4	cups all-purpose flour

3	teaspoons baking powder
1/2	teaspoon salt
1/2	cup milk

- In a large bowl, combine rhubarb and 1-1/2 cups sugar. Transfer to a greased 11-in. x 7-in. baking dish. Sprinkle with marshmallows.

- In a small bowl, cream the butter, vanilla and remaining sugar until light and fluffy. Combine the flour, baking powder and salt; add dry ingredients to the creamed mixture alternately with milk. Beat the mixture just until moistened; spoon over the rhubarb.

- Bake at 350° for 50-55 minutes or until the topping is golden brown. Serve warm.

YIELD: 10-12 SERVINGS.

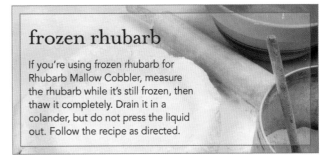

frozen rhubarb

If you're using frozen rhubarb for Rhubarb Mallow Cobbler, measure the rhubarb while it's still frozen, then thaw it completely. Drain it in a colander, but do not press the liquid out. Follow the recipe as directed.

GENERAL RECIPE INDEX

This index lists every recipe by major ingredients.
For specific types of pies, refer to the recipe list at the beginning of each chapter.

TASTE OF HOME BEST-LOVED PIES

ALPHABETICAL INDEX